D0485915

AN OUTLINE OF NEW TESTAMENT SPIRITUALITY

An Outline of
New Testament Spirituality

Prosper Grech, O.S.A.

William B. Eerdmans Publishing Company

Grand Rapids, Michigan / Cambridge, U.K.

© 2011 Prosper Grech
All rights reserved

Published 2011 by
Wm. B. Eerdmans Publishing Co.
2140 Oak Industrial Drive N.E., Grand Rapids, Michigan 49505 /
P.O. Box 163, Cambridge CB3 9PU U.K.
www.eerdmans.com

Printed in the United States of America

16 15 14 13 12 11   7 6 5 4 3 2 1

Library of Congress Cataloging-in-Publication Data

Grech, Prosper.
An outline of New Testament spirituality / Prosper Grech.
p.   cm.
ISBN 978-0-8028-6560-1 (pbk.: alk. paper)
1. Bible. N.T. — Criticism, interpretation, etc.
2. Spirituality — Biblical teaching.   I. Title.

BS2370.G74   2011
248 — dc22

2010045209

Unless otherwise noted, the Scripture quotations in this publication
are from the New Revised Standard Version Bible, copyright © 1989
by the Division of Christian Education of the National Council of
Churches of Christ in the U.S.A., and used by permission.

Contents

Preface

This outline contains what I consider to be the essential themes for meditation by all those — lay people, religious, and priests, of whatever confession — who seek to live their Christian faith in its fullness. I have tried to let the texts speak for themselves without complicating them with notes or long explanations, but as some kind of interpretation is indispensable, my running commentary follows the exegesis of approved scholars. I am well aware that I have had to ride roughshod over many disputed exegetical, theological, and historical problems, for which I beg the indulgence of the academy, but the main purpose of this book is to help the reader to respond to God's gift in Christ with love and discernment rather than to lecture him or her. If readers are using the *Outline* as a basis for group discussions it would be advisable to read in full the principal biblical texts referred to, and to consult some commentary or other to provide this scanty presentation with some more substance.

I am very grateful to Barnabas Johns who revised my typescript and made many useful suggestions, as well as to many colleagues who read it and encouraged its publication. Above all, my thanks go to Eerdmans Publishing Company for taking the risk of putting it into print.

Introduction

What do we mean by New Testament spirituality? The answer to this question will determine both the contents and the methodology of this book. The term "spirituality" is rather vague. Apart from the fact that it relates to all religions, when applied to the New Testament it must be further qualified unless we mean it to comprise the whole of New Testament theology. I take it to denote the Christian's total response of faith, made effective through love and vivified by the Holy Spirit, to God's self-manifestation in Christ. This interpretation distinguishes it, at least partially, from the kerygmatic aspect of theology that deals with the presentation of God's saving initiative through Christ in itself. It is more difficult to distinguish spirituality from moral teaching, though some authors would prefer to consider them identical. Moral theology is particularly concerned with what the Bible considers as right or wrong in our actions and attitudes. Spiritual theology, by contrast, penetrates deeply into the mystery of our redemption, and inquires about the completeness of our response of loving faith to God's gift in Christ. Christian spirituality includes detachment and self-discipline, as do many religions, and a transcendent vision, as do some philosophies, but the distinguishing feature of Christian spirituality is its relatedness to the Word's incarnation, which distinguishes it even from Jewish piety. Such spirituality describes and fosters the believer's total donation of self in response to God's total self-giving.

The methodological problems are not different from any other New Testament research. As far as possible, we examine texts for their literal meaning and in their original *Sitz im Leben*. This does not require from the Christian exegete a complete phenomenological detachment as if he were studying the Upanishads, because his faith requires a personal involvement in his reading. Yet the question arises whether biblical spirituality should be studied historically, as a thing of the past, or hermeneutically, as something existentially relevant to believers today. These two aspects are not mutually exclusive, but one must not forget that between the composition of the New Testament and today there are twenty centuries of interpretation and historical development, which hermeneutics must take into account to bridge the gap adequately.

I also face the decision as to whether to opt for a thematic exposition of the relevant material or to examine the Testament author by author. As this book is meant for believers who wish to deepen their spiritual lives, we shall follow a few themes from the Synoptic Gospels through the Pauline and Johannine writings. We begin by examining our existential situation: If we are to be "saved," from what are we to be saved? An overview of the spirituality inherited from the Old Testament follows, as this too forms part of the Christian's response to God's saving initiative. The teaching of Jesus, as interpreted by the Synoptic Gospels, is the foundation of the life of every believer. The fourth section deals with our incorporation into the Paschal mystery, the redeeming death and resurrection of Christ, especially in the letters of Paul and his school. Next comes the place of faith and love in the Gospel and letters of John, and we end with an assessment of the Christian's place within history and his or her hope of final redemption.

My approach is canonical; that is, I consider the New Testament as a whole in which one text can explain another even if it comes from a different author. In spite of the variety of theologies within the New Testament, there is coherence among the diverse responses of that faith common to all the writers who produced the New Testament, that faith which served later as a criterion for the formation of the canon.

An adequate reflection on all the relevant texts would necessitate many volumes. I therefore concentrate on those texts most essential for understanding our main argument.

1

Deliverance: From What? By Whom?

We are all attached to life and well-being and continually menaced by various evils: sickness, violence, loss of liberty, disasters, sadness, and finally, death. Even our happiest moments are blurred by a lingering subconscious anxiety. This is our undeniable existential situation. Any answer to the questions posed in the title of this chapter assumes our anthropological, cosmological, and theological nature. That this is not the best of worlds in which humanity exists is obvious. But why is it so? What can be done to render existence more acceptable?

An agnostic would say that these are queries to which there is no answer, so let's just make the best of it for tomorrow we will die. Siddhartha Gautama, however, understood the problem of suffering as being the foundation of Buddhism, and would say that because all evils arise from desire, the extinction of all desires leads to beatitude, or nirvana. In spite of its difficulty, he would say this is entirely within our capabilities and requires no recourse to any transcendent being. Hinduism also takes the problem seriously and seeks a resolution in the meditation of the Self (atman) as identical with the Transcendent Self (Brahman). In China, both Confucianism and Taoism base their ethics on the reaction to the evils within society at large. Primitive animistic religions are so beset with the problem of evil that witch-doctors act as their priests; and second-century Gnosticism, with its Platonic worldview, identified matter created by a demigod as being the source of all evil.

If these questions occupy such an important place in world religions and philosophies and give rise to such a multitude of "spiritualities," then what answer does the Bible give to such problems as the nature of humankind, the goodness of the world, the why of suffering, and the way out?

Scripture defines the human being in relation to God. We read that each human is God's creature: "Then God said, 'Let us make humankind in our image, according to our likeness. . . .' So God created humankind in his image, in the image of God he created them; male and female he created them. God blessed them, and God said to them: 'Be fruitful and multiply, and fill the earth and subdue it; and have dominion over the fish of the sea and over the birds of the air and over every living thing that moves upon the earth'" (Gen. 1:26-28). Adam's dominion over the earth and its creatures defines his being as an image and likeness of God himself: he can only subdue the earth if he shares in God's wisdom and in his freedom. He is neither part of God nor independent of him; like all other creatures he is brought into being from nothingness, which diminishes nothing of his dignity but prompts the psalmist to exclaim: "When I look at your heavens, the work of your fingers, the moon and the stars that you have established; what are human beings that you are mindful of them, mortals that you care for them? Yet you have made them a little lower than God, and crowned them with glory and honor" (Ps. 8:3-5). This is an anthropology based on faith in one God, the Creator, who made us in his own image and likeness to be able to enter into dialogue with him. Such a concept of the human being was not the fruit of philosophical reasoning or drawn from experience; in fact any consideration drawn from the ups and downs of daily living would hardly measure up to a quasi-divine being. Qohelet vividly describes the skepticism and cynicism into which we are all tempted to fall if we base our philosophy of life only on the contradictions of our ordinary contingencies.

The Bible is very realistic about our existential situation. The book of Job asks how to reconcile God's justice with the suffering of the righteous and ends by declaring our inability to penetrate this mystery (Job 42:1-6) without offering any way out except Job's confession of his ignorance of God's transcendent designs. The historical books too, notwithstanding their insistence on the call of the patriarchs, Moses, and the election of Israel, underline the slavery in Egypt, the raids of foreign peoples in the book of Judges, the exiles and other evils that befell Israel and Judah. Psalms 90 and 103 sum up humans' plight in a few verses: "The days of our life are seventy years, or perhaps eighty, if we are strong; even then their span is only toil and trouble; they are soon gone, and we fly away" (90:10); "As for mortals, their days are like grass; they flourish like a flower of the field; for the wind passes over it, and it is gone, and its place knows it no more" (103:15-16). Yet these existential ills of humanity are not recounted for their own sake, but only as a contrast to God's saving love; God is the ultimate redeemer.

The New Testament is no less aware of the sufferings of human beings. Jesus' healings and exorcisms, his mission to the poor, his pity on sinners, and the eschatological tone of his sayings express his concern regarding humanity's plight. He is the one who brings God's deliverance to humans.

There is no need to prolong the list of miseries; we are all well aware of them. They all pose the eternal problem of how we reconcile our faith in one good, just, merciful, and all-powerful God with suffering and death. The account of the creation in Genesis 1 ends with the apodictic statement: "God saw everything that he had made, and indeed, it was very good" (1:31). Does this make sense or must we presume that something has gone wrong in the course of history?

The biblical writer known as the Jahwist offers his answer in his narrative of the formation of Adam from the dust of the earth, made alive by God's breath, and his subsequent rebellion, constantly reiterated by his descendents until the hardening of heart touches rock bottom (Gen. 2–11). These narratives are "mythical" or "symbolical" in the sense that they never happened and yet happen continually. Yet though mythical and symbolical, the narratives are not therefore unhistorical, as alienation from God did have a historical beginning. Describing its origin by means of symbolical narratives enhances rather than diminishes the richness of theological significance. An exhaustive explanation of these chapters is outside the scope of this book, but we can try to decipher some of these symbols and translate them into comprehensible theological language.

In Genesis 2:4-6 the writer tells us that in the beginning, the earth was barren and treeless because there was no one to cultivate it. Man is created from the dust of this unfruitful earth, endowed with God's spirit of life (2:7), meaning matter and spirit, and placed in a luxuriant garden planted on purpose by God (2:8-14). The abundance of waters and the mention of gold and precious stones associated with Eden symbolize the amenities and richness of this environment as the Creator's gift to humankind and its state of beatitude intended by God. The symbols in Genesis 2 recall the state of chaos and darkness of the newly created universe described in chapter 1 and of the area of light segregated by God in which to build his world, with Adam as its master and carer (1:2, 28-29). Humankind's dominion, however, is not absolute; the prohibition to eat from the tree of the knowledge of good and evil (2:17) signifies humankind's subjection to the will of God in matters of right and wrong.

Adam "named" all the animals, indicating his superiority and dominion over them (2:19-20) but they could not act as consorts. Eve's formation out of a rib, the place closest to Adam's heart, is a parable about the attraction between male and female, and their intention to be reunited in marriage as a single personality (2:18-25).

Enter the serpent (3:1-7), with his crafty insinuations to subvert the order of creation and engender death. Wisdom 2:23 makes it clear that the serpent was none other than the devil, himself formerly part of God's good creation, but who, blinded by envy, rebelled against his Creator and now urges humans to reject their submission to God, declare their independence, and decide for themselves what is good or evil for them, thus thwarting God's pretense to subjugate them.

Woman and man eat of the forbidden fruit, trustingly expecting a marvelous metamorphosis into godhead, only to discover that they are naked (3:2-7): this is one of the most bitter paradoxes in all literatures. The author had already informed us that the couple was naked, but felt no shame, because, as later Jewish literature reflected, they had been clothed with God's glory; their present deprivation, recalled by Paul in Romans 3:23, opens their eyes to the nothingness of humankind when isolated from God. Their shame and mutual accusations are due to their sense of guilt (Gen. 3:8-13).

Now comes the punishment (3:14-19): no more amenities for males in a fruitful garden, they will have to struggle against the soil to earn a slice of bread, and after a life of toil man will return to the dust from which he was formed. Women are punished in their femininity: their greatest hour, that of childbearing, will be an hour of suffering, and their natural instinct towards the male will only lead them to subjection. The serpent's punishment, apart from the etiological explanation of his crouching in and feeding on dust in verse 14, is best quoted in full: "I will put enmity between you and the woman, and between your offspring and hers; he will strike your head, and you will strike his heel" (v. 15). This is a little apocalypse, the key to understanding the constant conflict within history between good and evil. Woman's offspring, humankind, is doomed to fall because of the wound in its heel, but in the end it is humans who will have the final victory by crushing the serpent's head. Revelation 12:9 takes up this motif to interpret Christ as that offspring who will finally cast down the "ancient serpent," Satan.

Then follows the expulsion from paradise (3:22-24): as paradise is not a "place" but a state of friendship and union with the Creator, expulsion means that God "hides his face from humans" (cf. Deut. 31:17; 32:20), depriving them of God's presence, so that humans, left alone but yearning for reunion, can only "grope for" God (Acts 17:27) in the hope of finding him.

The story of "original sin" does not end in Genesis 3, but continues through chapters 4 to 11. The social and moral consequences of humans' break with God are symbolized in the narratives about Cain and Abel (4:1-16): fratricide and internecine struggle, with the wicked wandering away ever further from God's presence; Lamech marries two wives in whose presence he boasts of his murders (4:19-24); Tubal-cain is responsible for the forging of weapons (4:22); sexual promiscuity provokes the deluge (6:1-13), and finally, Adam's ambition to rise to the stature of God repeats itself in the construction of the tower of Babel (ch. 11). Human behavior rolls down to rock bottom; if God does not intervene in some way or other the serpent will have the upper hand. St. Paul sums this up in Romans 5:12, 18, 21: "Sin came into the world through one man, and death came through sin, and so death spread to all because all have sinned. . . . Therefore just as one man's trespass led to condemnation for all, so one man's act of righteousness leads to justification and life for all. . . . just as sin exercised dominion in death, so grace might also exercise dominion through justification leading to eternal life through Jesus Christ our Lord."

The consequences of this initial breakaway from God, "the fountain of life" (Ps. 36:9) are multiple. Paul informs us that through Adam's transgression sin entered this world. There is some difference between the biblical and the theological sense of sin. We usually understand by this word what the Bible calls a transgression, that is, an act or thought contrary to God's law that renders us guilty before him. Moreover, the theologian distinguishes between the "original sin" initially committed by Adam and the "original sin" inherited by us all. This latter is usually explained as the lack of sanctifying grace in which we are born, because we belong to a humanity deprived of God's friendship, just as the descendants of a noble forefather who has been deprived of his title because of some crime or other themselves lack the title through no fault of their own; or like the forced sufferings of the citizens of a country whose dictatorial leader declares it to be at war. The biblical sense of sin does include that of transgression, but it usually denotes that compelling power which drives us to evil and to rebellion; the rabbis called this inclination to evil the *yetzer ha-ra*, which only the law could overcome. God's warning to Cain makes this clear: "Sin is lurking at the door; its desire is for you, but you must master it" (Gen. 4:7), and Paul's dramatic description in Romans 7 of the struggle within the human being between the desire to do good and the enslaving power of sin is even more dramatic. The internal freedom of the human being is constantly at stake in his present existential state.

As Adam had been warned, sin engenders death, and this term, too, is not univocal. It certainly denotes bodily death, the return to dust, against which the first man had been warned. Biological death, however, is a consequence of spiritual death, occurring through the soul's separation from the Fount of Life; but death also has a cosmic meaning, perhaps best understood as a power that continually threatens the order of creation itself. Humans are caught up in this strife between life and death. When we confess that Christ's resurrection overcame death we do not mean simply that he rose again personally, but that he has eschatologically vanquished the cosmic dominion of death, as Revelation 20:13-15 explains. Paul too, speaking of the resurrection, exclaims: "'Death has been swallowed up in victory.' 'Where, O death is your victory? Where, O death, is your sting?'" (1 Cor. 15:54-55).

A third power which constantly limits our freedom is "the world" — not the cosmos which had been declared "very good" at the beginning of creation, but that complex of errors, prejudices, vices, customs, and attitudes within our societies that determine our decisions and render it so difficult, if not impossible, for us to exist, to emerge, to be ourselves and follow the truth wherever it may lead. This is the usual sense of the word in the Johannine writings; Jesus encourages his disciples when he proclaims: "Take courage; I have conquered the world!" (John 16:33).

The "world" is "blind" because it cannot perceive the truth. John's detailed narrative of the healing of the man born blind in John 9 presents the Pharisees as an example of blindness and ends with Jesus' reproof: "If you were blind, you would not have sin. But now that you say, 'We see,' your sin remains" (9:41). Apart from physical lack of sight, blindness here means the ignorance and pride that renders us sightless even in the presence of clear evidence.

Another negative factor that must be purified is "the flesh." "Spirit" and "flesh" are not simply to be equated with "soul" and "body"; the biblical meaning of "flesh" is the whole person, body and soul, under the aspect of weakness, so even such incorporeal sins as pride and hatred belong to the realm of the flesh. "Spirit," on the other hand, is divine power strengthening humans to walk in the way of righteousness. Isaiah 31:3 warns the Israelites against relying on the military help of the Egyptian cavalry, whose horses are "flesh, and not spirit"; that is, place your trust in God, not in anything human. Paul associates flesh with the law and with sin when he says: "We know that the law is spiritual; but I am of the flesh, sold into slavery under sin. I do not understand my own actions. For I do not do what I want, but I do the very thing I hate. . . . For I know that nothing good dwells within me, that is, in my flesh. I can

8

will what is right, but I cannot do it" (Rom. 7:14-15, 18). This means that while the law certainly presents an ideal to be followed and our intellect perceives its goodness, the power of sin subdues us in our weakness, and, in spite of our good will, we follow the promptings of "the flesh." Yet God has equipped us for this challenge too: "The law of the Spirit of life in Christ Jesus has set you free from the law of sin and of death" (Rom. 8:2).

If we now turn to Jesus' miracles we reflect on other evils of which we are all well aware: illnesses, cosmic catastrophes, and the domination of the evil one. The miracles can be classified into three categories: healings; exorcisms; and interventions in nature, such as raising the dead, walking on the waters, calming storms, and multiplying loaves of bread. These are not mere acts of beneficence though they certainly did benefit the recipients, who were only a minute fraction of all those who needed help. Rather, John calls the miracles "signs," for a sign points to something beyond itself, an end to be reached. The key to their symbolic meaning is to be found in Old Testament symbolism. Thus the miracles worked by Jesus in the presence of the Baptist's disciples in Matthew 11:5 recall Isaiah 35:5 foretelling the wonders which would take place in eschatological times, hence indicating Jesus as the awaited Messiah. Mark's Gospel abounds in exorcisms, stressing Christ's final victory over Satan, the source of all evil, while such wonders as the multiplication of loaves or the calming of a storm recall the manna in the desert and God's domination over the chaos of history in traditional biblical imagery. It is John, however, who best explains in which sense these miracles are signs. If Jesus opens the eyes of a blind man he proclaims himself as the light of the world (9:5); when he raises Lazarus he says, "I am the resurrection and the life" (11:25); and after the multiplication of loaves he asserts that he is the bread of life (6:35). Significantly, each saying is followed by a confession of faith on the part of the witnesses. As the Fourth Gospel must be read on both the historical level and on the level of the risen Christ, the miracles worked on a few people two thousand years ago in a definite place point to the incessant spiritual activity of the Lord in his exalted state and require faith on the part of all those who turn to him to enter the role of participants.

The narratives in Genesis 1–11 and the biblical terminology of the moral and existential consequences of the fall should not be read only on the individual and personal level, for they have social repercussions which, read hermeneutically, contribute in no mean manner to contemporary social and environmental discussions. Humankind's original state of dominion over nature and the rebellion of the land outside paradise can provide some answers to our ecological problems. The subjection of woman to her consort after the fall, the racial differences hinted at in the narrative about Shem, Ham, and Japheth after the deluge, and the differences between Jews and non-Jews that we see all through the Old Testament find their New Testament answer in Paul's apodictic statement: "There is no longer Jew or Greek, there is no longer slave or free, there is no longer male and female; for all of you are one in Christ Jesus" (Gal. 3:28).

Up to this point we have tried to answer the first part of the question posed in the title of this chapter: Deliverance from what? The reply to the second question — Deliverance by whom? — should now be evident. We have enumerated the existential evils that threaten humankind's quest for happiness as found in Scripture. The fundamental biblical doctrine in answer to the second question is that humanity is unable to save itself by its own strength unless God stretches out an arm to lift up humans from their misery. Self-sufficiency is the negation of faith as much as fatalism is the surrender of initiative and responsibility.

The meanings of the words "salvation," "redemption," and "liberation" overlap; in both the Old and New Testaments the main savior, redeemer, or liberator from the evils besetting humankind is God, or the Father through Jesus Christ. A few examples contrasting human weakness with God's power demonstrate this. It is

Yahweh who saves Israel from Egyptian bondage, who offers the covenant, who raises the "judges" to free the tribes from foreign incursions, from the Babylonian exile and other national calamities. In Isaiah 40–66 salvation assumes a more spiritual sense and the hope of a final act of salvation is intensified. When Yahweh makes use of humans as agents of liberation, God chooses the weakest to make it evident that his people are founded on his own power, lest pride should tempt them to do without him. God, therefore, is the absolute Giver; our relationship with God is one of faith, which is the acknowledgment that everything we have comes from God and a response of gratitude translated into the holiness of daily life. Paul's description of his own interior struggle ends with an exclamation which sums up all we have been trying to say in this chapter: "Wretched man that I am! Who will rescue me from this body of death? Thanks be to God through Jesus Christ our Lord!" (Rom. 7:24-25).

2

Response to the Old Testament Covenant: An Inherited Piety

Jesus was a Jew, and so were the apostles and the earliest believers in Christ. They never renounced their Judaism, they only "updated" it, asserting its total fulfillment in the manifestation of the kingdom of God foretold by the prophets. All of them continued living a pious life according to Jewish faith and customs; what distinguished them from other Jews was their faith that Jesus was the Christ who rose from the dead and poured down on them the Holy Spirit promised in the Scriptures. Their Christian piety was their old Jewish response to God's gift reviewed in light of the recent saving events.

The essential characteristics of a pious Jew, at least in later Judaism, were belief in the one and only God and abhorrence of idol worship, conviction that God had chosen Israel from among all peoples, loyalty to the covenant, observance of Moses' law and the practices of prayer, fasting, and almsgiving. Illustrations of these attitudes and beliefs are scattered throughout the whole of the Old Testament, but I turn to the book of Psalms as the most suitable example of true Jewish piety. There are many reasons for this choice: the Psalter has various authors; it spans a long period of time; it is not primarily a book about God but springs from the believer's intimate relationship and dialogue with God; it is a response to God's gift and thus it portrays the doubts and struggles in the heart of the supplicant in his existential situation here and now. Some Christians are loath to recite the psalms because they consider as unchristian the hatred of enemies often expressed in them. I explain at the end of this chapter how to "baptize" the psalms and the reason why the church continues to make constant use of these beautiful hymns in her daily prayers.

The psalms are a model of spirituality because they give voice to the response of believers, guided by the Spirit, to God's self-manifestation in creation, in Israel's history, in his holy temple, in the anointed King, in gratitude for deliverance from national and personal calamities, and they do so through the psalmist's search for God, in his doubts, in his repentance, in his observance of the law, and in his hopes for the future. We shall examine each of these moods and dispositions and provide a few illustrations from these poetic prayers.

"O LORD, our Sovereign, how majestic is your name in all the earth! You have set your glory above the heavens. . . . When I look at your heavens, the work of your fingers, the moon and the stars that you have established; what are human beings that you are mindful of them?" (Ps. 8:1, 3-4). Such marvel runs through many of these canticles: Psalms 65 and 148 speak of the rain, meadows, flocks, the stars, the mountains, and the seas. All this beauty reveals God's wisdom (136:1-9): "All the gods of the peoples are idols, but the LORD made the heavens. Honor and majesty are before him; strength and beauty are in his sanctuary" (96:5-6). It is as if the whole universe were God's temple, epitomized in the place of worship on Mount Zion. Idol worship is not only senseless; it also affronts Israel's self-consciousness as the upholder of monotheism. Psalm 104 describes in detail the methodical order of creation, in which times and seasons play their own part to maintain all living creatures, kept alive by the spirit of a God who is so transcendent that if he but looks down the heavens tremble, and at whose touch the mountains smoke. It is precisely this unique omnipotence of the Creator that proclaims him also as the Lord of history (Ps. 147), in which Israel's mission to the nations finds its proper place.

The pious Israelite's contemplation does not limit itself to the marvels of creation, but extends to how God manifests his love in the events of the nation's history. The exodus, of course, was considered as the founding occurrence in Israel's life. God had shown his power over the Egyptians and over all peoples who threatened the existence of his people during their wanderings in the desert; it was not their military might but Yahweh's mighty hand that led them into the Promised Land. The conviction about these events gave birth to Israel's consciousness of being one people, under God's ownership. No wonder therefore that the psalms so often commemorate this unique occurrence.

Psalm 136 is a thanksgiving litany that begins with praises of God the Creator and then goes on to enumerate God's wonders from the exodus to the possession of the Promised Land. Psalm 78 is a link in the chain of transmission of Yahweh's deeds from generation to generation so that the descendants of the psalmist may give thanks to God and never cease to hope in him in times of difficulty and distress. They should not imitate their forebears in the desert, however, who were stubborn and tempted God by means of their unbelief. Therefore, Psalm 105 goes further and attributes God's merciful rescue of the people from Egypt to his covenant with Abraham and Jacob, which promised the possession of the land of Canaan (v. 11). The stories of Joseph and the plagues on Egypt are related, as are the Lord's saving actions during the Israelites' wanderings in the desert. The appeal to the Abrahamic covenant is a message to those who thought that God owed these wonders to the Israelites because of their goodness: rather, Yahweh favored them for the sake of his own holy name, their infidelities notwithstanding.

The awareness of Yahweh's ongoing guidance of Israel's history extends beyond the exodus to the covenant with David. Psalm 89 was composed when the Davidic succession was threatened with extinction, probably at the time of the exile. The psalmist reminds God of his promise that David should have an unbroken line of successors forever, he recalls Yahweh's defeat of chaotic powers symbolized by the raging seas, and he asks that God keep his promise and save God's anointed. In spite of contrary evidence, the psalmist is certain that the Lord of history and the Father of the Davidic line will keep his word.

A moving prayer is Psalm 44, which contrasts Yahweh's wondrous deeds as recounted by the ancestors with the present plight of the people in exile. The psalmist has not lost faith nor given up his hope, and he ends with the anguished cry: "Rouse yourself! Why do you sleep, O Lord? Awake, do not cast us off forever! Why do you hide your face? Why do you forget our affliction and oppression? For we sink down to the dust; our bodies cling to the ground. Rise up, come to our help. Redeem us for the sake of your steadfast love" (vv. 23-26).

The proper place to contemplate God's presence, however, is the Jerusalem temple, towards which processions of pilgrims ascend singing Psalms 120–134. In 1 Kings 8:10 we read that during the consecration of Solomon's temple the glory of the Lord took possession of the holy place and rested in the form of a cloud upon the Ark of the Covenant. Solomon's subsequent prayer stressed the fact that in spite of the whole earth belonging to Yahweh he chose to reside in this temple to listen to the prayers of the faithful and grant their requests. This event is recalled in Psalm 24, which prescribes the purity of soul required to enter God's house, and sings the refrain: "Lift up your heads, O gates! and be lifted up, O ancient doors! that the King of glory may come in. Who is this King of glory? The LORD of hosts, he is the King of glory" (24:9-10).

It is Psalm 27, however, that best expresses the pious Jew's sentiments within the temple. His trust in God prevails over the threat of his enemies, and it is in the temple that he finds all this courage: "One thing I asked of the LORD, that will I seek after: to live in the house of the LORD all the days of my life, to behold the beauty of the LORD, and to inquire in his temple. For he will hide me in his shelter in the day of trouble; he will conceal me under the cover of his tent" (vv. 4-5b). An impulse of love within his heart makes the psalmist cry: "Your face, LORD, do I seek. Do not hide your face from me. . . . I believe that I shall see the goodness of the LORD in the land of the living" (vv. 8b-9, 13). To behold God's face is to experience God's loving-kindness. The expectation to see the goodness of God in the land of the living in the Jewish context means deliverance from death, but in a later setting, when the belief in Sheol made way for the hope of resurrection, these verses were read with this new meaning.

Psalm 50 makes it clear that the authentic cult of Yahweh in the temple does not consist merely of ritual sacrifices of animals; verses 14-15 insist on a spirit of thanksgiving, on the rendering of vows and on trust in God; the wicked who do not accompany their ritual with a pure heart only bring punishment upon themselves (vv. 16-22). The disappointment and sorrow of the writer of Psalm 79 at the destruction of the temple is therefore understandable. Not only is his cry, "How long, O LORD? Will you be angry forever?" (v. 5) motivated by his concern with the dimming of God's honor among the Gentiles: "Why should the nations say, 'Where is their God?'" (v. 10), but also in his desire in the hope for retribution, in hopes that Yahweh's sovereignty over the whole world be acknowledged.

The pious Israelite can contemplate God's splendor also in the king's majesty. Psalms 2 and 110, composed by a court poet on the occasion of the king's enthronement but later reread with reference to the King Messiah, consider the sovereign as God's lieutenant whose victory over the nations acquires an apocalyptic significance. The ideal king, according to Psalm 72, is endowed with justice, righteousness, and glory; peace and prosperity flourish during his reign. In the history of both Israel and Judah there were few ideal kings; no wonder, therefore, that even this psalm was projected into the future and referred to the Messiah. The celebration of a royal wedding sung in Psalm 45 praises not only the power of the king but also the beauty of the queen, and foretells the greatness of her offspring. In pre-exilic Jerusalem, king and temple are correlative, so God's glory can be contemplated in both.

Many psalms are prayers for deliverance, both personal and national. They belong to the genre of lament. The use of the singular "I" in some of these psalms probably indicates that the prayer was composed as an individual request, but was soon taken up by the community and the "I" becomes a "we," often within the same poem. The evils from which the suppliant asks God to deliver him are some of those listed in the previous chapter. Illness and death are often mentioned together with the hypocrisy and hatred of the suppliant's enemies or false friends, as in Psalm 41. These psalms frequently include not only a confession of sinfulness but also of trust in God's mercy in the same lament. Some call to mind the book of Job. Persecution by enemies and betrayal by false friends, as in the case of the alternation between first person singular and plural, may refer either to personal affliction or to the whole nation, socially or politically. The sufferer is sometimes a poor man oppressed by the rich; both Psalm 49 and Psalm 52 belong to this category and explain very clearly what is meant by "rich" and "poor" with reference to the self-assurance engendered by ephemeral power and affluence to create one's felicity, at the expense of the poor. Only trust in God and almsgiving qualify as piety. The suppliant in Psalm 56 uses moving words to vent his feelings: "You have kept count of my tossings; put my tears in your bottle. Are they not in your record?" (v. 8). The pious pauper prostrates himself humbly before God and makes known his confidence in the Lord "like a weaned child with its mother" (Ps. 131:2). Even psalms with such strong a cry of anguish as "My God, my God, why have you forsaken me?" (22:1) cited by Jesus on the cross, end with words of hope and praise.

If we now probe more closely into the pious Israelite's vocabulary in his more intimate moments of prayer we discover a great richness of emotions, warmth, and fervor which sometimes borders on mystical experience. The author of the well-known Psalm 23 calls the Lord his shepherd and likens himself to a sheep lying down in green pastures, led to brooks of pure water, comforted by the rod and staff of his pastor, and banqueting at a rich table in the presence of his enemies. He is certain to dwell in the house of the Lord, that is, in his intimate friendship, all the days of his life. The word "love," on God's part as well as on the petitioner's, appears quite often in this literature, as do various expressions of joy (such as Ps. 86:11-13). It is Psalm 139, however, that best reveals a human's transparency in God's eyes. God knows our most intimate thoughts even before we conceive them and all our ways and sentiments, because it was God who formed us and knit us together within our mother's womb. It is impossible to hide or escape from God, for God is and sees everywhere. The prayer concludes with a submissive request: "Search me, O God, and know my heart; test me and know my thoughts. See if there is any wicked way in me, and lead me in the way everlasting" (vv. 23-24).

Words expressing the believer's longing for God are no less touching. "My soul thirsts for you like a parched land" (143:6); "As a deer longs for flowing streams, so my soul longs for you, O God. My soul thirsts for God, for the living God. When shall I come and behold the face of God?" (42:1-2); "O God . . . my flesh faints for you, as in a dry and weary land where there is no water" (63:1); "O taste and see that the LORD is good; happy are those who take refuge in him" (34:8).

We find colorful metaphors describing God's protection and saving presence. They are obviously anthropomorphisms — but the invisible Yahweh must be imagined in some way or other. Though no one can behold God's "face," yet this aspect of God's closeness is often referred to in the psalms. God invites us to "seek his face" (27:8); the just man beholds his face, which usually means seeking his grace in humble faith (11:7; 17:15). When Yahweh makes the light of his face shine upon someone, his smile fills the petitioner with joy and prosperity (4:6; 67:1). When the Lord hides his face, that is, when he does not answer the psalmist's prayers, the pious man feels rejected and cries louder to be heard and accepted (88:14; 27:9). A parallel expression is God's "silence" (83:1). By contrast, when God hides his face from the wicked, he rejects their prayers and leaves them to their own fate (34:16) but when God hides his face from our sins that is a sign of forgiveness (51:9). It is in the temple that the faithful seek to contemplate the face of the Most High: God's saving presence.

Another eloquent anthropomorphism is the phrase "God's wings." God is imagined as a huge bird in the shadow of whose wings the poor and oppressed can find shelter. The expression recalls the Spirit of God hovering over the waters of chaos in Genesis 1:2. In the psalms protection and salvation are sought: "Guard me as the apple of your eye; hide me in the shadow of your wings" (17:8). A verse which brings together various significant metaphors is Psalm 36:7 "How precious is your steadfast love, O God! All people may take refuge in the shadow of your wings. They feast on the abundance of your house, and you give them drink from the river of your delights. For with you is the fountain of life; in your light we see light." Here, love, abundance, refuge under God's wings, a draught from the river of delight which springs from the fountain of life, and the human's illumination by the light of God's countenance are brought together as equivalent terms. Life and light are correlatives as in the prologue of John's Gospel: "In him [the Word] was life, and the life was the light of all people" (John 1:4). The writer of Psalm 27 confesses: "The LORD is my light and my salvation; whom shall I fear?" (v. 1). All these expressions can be summed up in the phrase "divine saving grace," to which the suppliant's piety is the response.

Jewish spirituality also contemplates God in the greatness as well as in the poverty of humankind. Psalm 8, to which we have already made an allusion, expresses wonder that the human person who, compared with the greatness of the universe is so minute, should be endowed with such glory and lavished with so much care that his status is merely a little lower than that of the *elohim* (= angels or God). On the other hand, when it comes to presenting one's sinfulness and misery before God the psalmist insists that his life is a mere passing breath or shadow (39:5-6; 144:3-4). Psalm 90:2-6 uses the words "dust," "a dream," and "fading grass" to justify the supplication for mercy and deliverance.

This obviously leads us to the consideration of our sinfulness. The psalms assert that no one is righteous or just before God (143:2), that all are corrupt: "The LORD looks down from heaven on humankind to see if there are any who are wise, who seek after God. They have all gone astray, they are all alike perverse; there is no one who does good, no, not one" (14:2-3). Repentance and prayer for forgiveness are the only remedies. Psalms 25, 103, and 130 are but a few that belong to this genre, but it is Psalm 51, the *Miserere*, that best expresses the feelings of the repentant sinner. The penitent can only appeal to gratuitous mercy and steadfast love, not to retributive justice (v. 1), for he acknowledges that he has no rights before God. In a tribunal he can only plead guilty, the prosecutor is simply right (v. 4). His only attenuating circumstance is that he was born of a sinful race (v. 5). This notwithstanding he begs for total cleansing and forgiveness (v. 2) as well as for help to be able to amend his ways in full sincerity, for only the gift of wisdom that can lead to righteousness (v. 6). The pronouncement of pardon will gladden his heart and fill it with joy (v. 8). Verses 10-12 recall Ezekiel 36:25-27, the favors to be poured upon Israel in the renewed covenant for the sake of God's holy name: the creation of a new, purified heart, and the gift of God's Spirit without which no righteousness can be attained. From being a sinner he can now become an apostle to others who still find themselves in his former plight (v. 13). If he ascends to the temple to offer a sacrifice for sin, he is aware that it is not the material victim that achieves forgiveness: "The sacrifice acceptable to God is a broken spirit; a broken and contrite heart, O God, you will not despise" (v. 17).

Until the second century BCE, there was no hope of any blessed future life in Israel. The dead merely descended into Sheol, the Greek Hades, where they lived on indistinctly as shades. This explains the insistence of a sick or persecuted man to be saved from death, from Sheol (cf. 16:9-11), although glimmers of hope of some kind of afterlife began to appear and were later made explicit. The desire to live a righteous life, therefore, was not for future recompense, but simply to remain within the covenant and thus to participate fully in God's blessings upon his people: "The LORD is my portion" (119:57).

Observing the Mosaic law was essential for remaining within the covenant. The long alphabetical Psalm 119 is a hymn to the law, in which the righteous sufferer protests his innocence to God and confesses that the law is the true and only pedagogue. This psalm belongs to the wisdom genre, and it is not the only one to exhort to virtue with promises of blessing on the righteous and the threat of punishment on sinners. The ideal answer to God's summons is "Here I am; in the scroll of the book it is written of me. I delight to do your will, O my God; your law is within my heart" (40:7). The wisdom sayings in the psalms, however, are only a fraction of the wisdom literature in the Old Testament. While the Torah prescribed the conditions for the observance of the covenant, such books as Proverbs, Ben Sirach, Job, and Wisdom were based on existential life-experience in the light of God's presence. The wisdom genre was common among all peoples in the ancient Near East and provided a suitable ground for what today we call inter-religious dialogue.

Yahweh was the only God of Israel, but he was actually God of the whole world, and Jewish prayer called on all nations to worship him: "Let the peoples praise you, O God; let all the peoples praise you. Let the nations be glad and sing for joy, for you judge the peoples with equity and guide the nations upon earth. . . . May God continue to bless us; let all the ends of the earth revere him" (67:3, 4, 7),

Each psalm was composed in a definite time and place in Israel's history; each one refers to a particular situation in the life of the poet or in the current historical circumstance of the nation. They were continually sung, however, and later generations recited the same words as earlier ones, applying them to their own personal or national situation. The meaning of these psalm texts is broader than the original author's vision and it is the change in social, historical, and religious circumstances that suggests this constant reinterpretation. A psalm reread after centuries has been enriched in the meantime by a growing tradition created by prophetic oracles, by sorrowful and joyful experiences, as well as by changes in the people's fortunes. The guidance of God's Spirit in the progress of revelation gives the canticle ever-new meanings. The key to this hermeneutical process is the manner in which the text addresses the reader, as an individual or as a congregation, with his or their particular needs, problems, and emotions.

As we noticed above, Christians inherited the psalms from the synagogue. The church sang them throughout the ages, often disengaging them from their original connotations and infusing them with new meanings. The liturgy sometimes applies the traditional words to the feast of the day. All is reread in the light of the Christ event. It is understandable that a contemporary follower of the gospel finds repugnant certain expressions of hatred and enmity; and he or she can also be perplexed by phrases referring to bygone ages that now seem meaningless. I shall therefore try in this section to provide some suggestions of how to "trans-late" the psalm from a Jewish linguistic milieu into a Christian perspective.

Our review of Jewish piety in the psalms concentrated on the diverse factors that led to the contemplation of God and the response to God's saving presence. While many psalms can be imported wholesale into Christian attitudes of prayer, others need some kind of transposition. That the believer in Christ contemplates God in the beauty of his creation need not be stressed; indeed, our modern view of the universe, ranging from the millions of light-years of its breadth to the mysteries of the atom, accentuates God's transcendence. On the other hand, we must update the Israelite's gratitude for God's intervention in the exodus and in multiple historical vicissitudes. We, too, thank God for having delivered the Israelites from their bondage in Egypt and for having preserved their identity throughout the ages, but the history of God's people did not end with the coming of Christ. The first Christians always considered themselves as the continuation of Israel, even after their repulse from the synagogue. The Christian exodus is essentially the Paschal mystery. The Eucharist, as a memory of the Last Supper, recalls the Jewish Passover. In his narrative of the Transfiguration, Luke relates that Jesus, Moses, and Elijah spoke of the departure or exodus which Christ was to accomplish in Jerusalem (Luke 9:31). In 1 Corinthians 10:1-11 Paul warns some Corinthians who compromised with idol worship that just as God had been severe with those who trespassed in the desert, so too will he not tolerate any similar transgression on the part of Christians. God's way of acting in the past, therefore, is transposed analogically to his relationship with the church, and to the Spirit's guidance of the New Israel (cf. Heb. 3:7-19). Hence the Christian also experiences divine guidance in the vicissitudes of church history, both negative and positive.

We saw above that God's grandeur could be contemplated in

the magnificence of the Jerusalem temple and of the Davidic king. The temple no longer exists, but we have another temple. In the episode of the cleansing of the temple Jesus said: "Destroy this temple, and in three days I will raise it up." John comments: "But he spoke of the temple of his body" (John 2:18-21). The Epistle to the Hebrews transposes the high priesthood and the ceremonies on the Day of Atonement to Christ's passion and death (5:5-10) and the ancient visible temple to the heavenly temple in which the risen Christ exercises his priesthood (9:11-12). Paul calls his Corinthian community God's temple (1 Cor. 3:16-17) and the whole church the body of Christ (1 Cor. 12; Rom. 12). The two metaphors of Christ as body and as temple were in common usage among the early believers and were commented on frequently by the Fathers.

As to the reflection of God's splendor on the King/Messiah, Psalms 2 and 110, which were originally coronation poems but later assumed a messianic meaning, are so often cited in the New Testament as to become part of the "book of testimonies," a written or oral collection of Old Testament texts of which the early church made common use. Jesus makes a solemn declaration that he is King before Pontius Pilate (John 18:33-37), with the proviso that his kingship is not of this world. In the Roman Empire, the status of the emperor was frequently proclaimed or re-proclaimed after some major victory over his enemies. His role was not merely home government but also the defense and extension of the empire. It is in these terms that Paul describes the kingship of the risen Christ in 1 Corinthians: "For he must reign until he has put all his enemies under his feet. The last enemy to be destroyed is death. For 'God has put all things in subjection under his feet.' . . . When all things are subjected to him, then the Son himself will also be subjected to him who put all things in subjection under him, so that God may be all in all" (15:25-28). This kind of language reminds us of a later episode when Titus subjected Judea and led the procession of captives and booty along the *via sacra* to the Capitol to present them to his father Vespasian, whom he later succeeded on the throne. The scriptural quotation in Paul's passage is from Psalm 110. We can extend our reinterpretation further by saying that as the pious Jew could see God's glory reflected in that of the King-Messiah, the Christian can speak of contemplating "the glory of God in the face of Jesus Christ" (2 Cor. 4:6). It is in this key that the royal psalms must be read by those who proclaim the kingship of the risen Christ.

The subjection of foes logically leads us to explain the loathing of enemies so frequently encountered in the canticles. These can be personal, social, or national enemies. The implicit assumption is that the enemy of a just man, of the poor, or of the nation is consequently also God's enemy, and so the psalmist invokes his punishment. The Christian who takes seriously the Sermon on the Mount with its injunction to love our enemies, to do good to those who harm us, and to pray for those who persecute us (Matt. 5:44) will find the cursing psalms repugnant. Is there any way of "christening" these prayers? The author of Revelation is no less lenient to the enemies of his churches than the suppliants in the Old Testament temple. It is precisely the genre to which Revelation belongs that will provide us with a hermeneutical key to be able to recite our psalms with a clear conscience and to insert our prayer into the theology of the kingdom of God.

The ancient prophet was someone with his feet firmly on the ground, well aware of what was happening in the political, social, and religious spheres. Like an editorial writer who writes the leading article in a newspaper from the political angle of his paper, the prophet preached or wrote about events around him from God's point of view, passing judgment, threatening, praising, or delivering messages of hope. The apocalyptic writer, on the other hand, in spite of his awareness of the real contemporary situation, looked up to heaven and interpreted his historical situation as a struggle between good and evil, foretelling the victory of God over adverse powers, to a group, often under stress or persecution, who could understand his symbolical language. Israel was a small nation placed between two great ones, the Egyptian and the Mesopotamian empires, and surrounded by other smaller countries often at war with one another or with the Jews; politically speaking these were the Israelite's "enemies." Within Israel, however, the rich, unjust judges, or the ruling class oppressed the poor, who cried to God for deliverance from their enemies. As in any other contingency there were also personal enmities with the weaker succumbing to the stronger. This is the life situation of the numerous psalms that cry for deliverance from the adversary and invoke God's intervention and punishment on the enemy.

If we now try to translate these prayers into Christian language, an apocalyptic view of history will be necessary. It would be tempting and easy to consider the enemy as the adversaries of the church, but the struggle is not between the church and non-Christians or other denominations, but between the "mystery of iniquity" (2 Thess. 2:7, KJV) and the mystery of salvation. This conflict can be found both within and outside the church, and is experienced even within the individual. The Christian's "enemies," therefore, are all those evils listed in the previous chapter from which we desire and beg deliverance. They are around us and within us. It is not "the enemy" we want destroyed — a believer prays for such a person — but the "mystery of evil" operating within him or her or within ourselves. In other words, we hate sin and not the sinner. Hence no triumphal exclamations, but the humble prayer: "Hallowed be thy name, thy kingdom come, thy will be done." Such an attitude makes sense of these imprecations, and, rather than creating boundaries and divisions between Christians and non-Christians it helps us to discern between the mystery of good and evil operative in society at large and in each individual. The psalms, which invite all nations to know and praise Yahweh, spur us on to evangelization and dialogue with all those in whom we perceive the work of the mystery of salvation. "The last enemy to be destroyed is death," says Paul (1 Cor. 15:26; see Rev. 20:14), death in its cosmic meaning as the destructive force in creation, under the power of the evil one.

The psalms expressing our personal relationship with God, and all those supplications arising from a deep and sincere desire to behold and experience God's presence, rather than themselves needing interpretation, interpret the Christian's noblest sentiments. No difficulty either in the recitation of the wisdom and the penitential psalms; the church sings the *miserere* every Friday at lauds. Its words are taken up by each individual and the ecclesial community itself: *simul iustus et peccator*.

A last observation concerns the legal genre, especially Psalm 119, in praise of the Mosaic law. The Christian who recites such expressions as himself being just and others sinners will fear that he is assuming the same air of superiority as the Pharisee in the temple who praised himself and despised the publican (Luke 18:9-14). First of all it would be of help to substitute "gospel" for "law." A hymn in praise of gospel values fits in better within a Christian assembly, but can anyone ever claim that he is a perfect observer of the gospel? We can only repeat these words with a clear conscience if we remember that in the Christian assembly the primary Orator is Christ as head of his body, the church: "You alone are the Holy One," we sing in the *gloria*. He is the gospel, so all phrases denoting self-praise must refer to him, the confession of deficiencies to ourselves.

As long as the church is still under construction it is imperative to keep in mind that, "Unless the LORD builds the house, those who build it labor in vain. Unless the LORD guards the city, the guard keeps watch in vain" (Ps. 127:1).

The Jewish response to the covenant leads to the Christian's response to the New Covenant.

3

Response to the Gift of the Kingdom: Jesus

The spiritual life of the Christian describes a person's continual progress in response to God's grace. The fundamental gift is the kingdom of heaven of which Jesus of Nazareth is the "sacrament." Our involvement in this mystery is proportionate to the depth of understanding and faith we can acquire through meditation and prayer on Jesus' person, message, and deeds. In this chapter we shall examine the Synoptic Gospels, themselves a witness of faith in and an interpretation of the chain of tradition that goes back to Jesus himself. This is not a form-critical study in the sense of trying to go back to his tape-recorded sayings and filmed activities; we take for granted the sincerity and authority of Matthew's, Mark's, and Luke's interpretative narratives as part and parcel of the church's tradition, handed down for the purpose of our sanctification. It is obviously impossible to go through all Jesus' words and deeds; we must be content to group them under a few headings, choose the most characteristic, and place them in order to facilitate a prayerful reflection on the requirements of the gospel message.

What Is the Kingdom?

Jesus' sayings and parables liken the kingdom to something or other and concentrate on how the listeners should respond to God's invitation to form part of this kingdom; its essential nature, however, is never defined. It sometimes appears as present (Luke 17:20-21), at other times as future, as when we pray for its coming (Matt. 6:10). The kingdom is other-worldly in Jesus' promise to the penitent robber (Luke 23:42-43), but in Mark 4:26-28 it appears as something growing within history. In Matthew's parable of the marriage feast (22:1-14) it is almost identified with the church; on the other hand, the kingdom promised in the Beatitudes (Matt. 5:3-11) refers to individuals or social groups. Each of these various facets has its own relevance, but when it comes to harmonizing them to describe the kingdom in its wholeness any kind of definition will always be unsatisfactory.

A further difficulty is the translation of the Greek word *basileia* used in the Gospels, or *malkut* in Hebrew. Each of these terms can refer to a king's sovereign power, to his kingdom as territory, or to the period of his reign. Expressions like "enter into the kingdom," "Thy kingdom come," or "The kingdom is near" need various additional words to be translated properly according to the context in which they are used. In its meaning as sovereignty, the kingdom entails power, and not merely juridical power but also a forceful energy: Jesus' miracles, symbols of the kingdom, are called *dynameis*, for a power issues from him (Mark 5:30). Some of the disciples will not see death till they behold the kingdom coming with power (Mark 9:1). In spite of these difficulties, it is at least useful to risk some kind of description or definition, however imprecise, as a working hypothesis, to be able to illustrate the spiritual response Jesus requires. The coming of the kingdom would comprise God's gratuitous offer of pardon and friendship to those who repent; his "taking matters in hand" to reorder a disoriented world towards the purpose for which it was created; the defeat of the powers of evil; the gathering into his domain of those who respond with faith and are endowed with power to spread his word; and, lastly, the judgment through the "Son of Man" on a resurrected humanity and the dwelling of the just in his paradise. This interpretation of the kingdom brings together Mark's insistence on the defeat of Satan, Matthew's view of the community of believers, Luke's emphasis on the spread of the gospel, Paul's idea of the gift of righteousness, and John's rewording of the kingdom as eternal life, here and hereafter. These various aspects will emerge here and there in the texts to be instanced. Jesus is the "sacrament" of the kingdom insofar as he, his miracles, his preaching, and his obedience unto death are visible signs of the Father's definitive initiative to save humankind from its alienation from divine friendship, a new beginning sealed by Jesus' resurrection from the dead.

The enigmatic nature of the kingdom results from the literary genre in which it was announced, the parable. The gospel parables are stories or similitudes taken from the common daily life of fishermen and peasants. The logic of the narrative is quite normal at the beginning but turns queer as the story unfolds: Which bridegroom would shut out the friends of the bride because they arrived late? Who would refuse an invitation to the wedding of the king's son? Or how does the dinner carry on undisturbed despite the siege of a city? The irruption of the powers of the kingdom does not follow human logic. Hence, the listener of a parable enters the scene as a common spectator, a third person, but with the unfolding of the narration he comes in as an actor and begins to take part for or against the various characters, praising or condemning, to find out, at the end, that he is actually condemning himself. An excellent example of this is Nathan's parable to the adulterer David after the king had sent Bathsheba's husband to his death (2 Sam. 12:1-13). The parable can sometimes be described as a linguistic net to trap the listener to admit his own faults. The reaction may be positive if the hearer is humble enough to mirror himself and admit his weakness, or it may be one of anger at being discovered and ends up in his smashing of the mirror, which was actually Jesus' fate. So why speak in parables rather than in plain words? Jesus gives the reason: "To you has been given the secret of the kingdom of God, but for those outside, everything comes in parables; in order that 'they may indeed look, but not perceive, and may indeed listen, but not understand; so that they may not turn again and be forgiven'" (Mark 4:11-12). Matthew's parallel saying is a little softer (Matt. 13:13). Parables are not meant as theological statements; they function every time they are heard or read, so it is the narrative itself that is the core of the teaching. Our whole life is a parable and events around us are merely "signs of the times," which Christians may interpret or ignore to their own benefit or detriment.

"Now after John was arrested, Jesus came to Galilee, proclaiming the good news of God, and saying, 'The time is fulfilled, and the kingdom of God has come near; repent, and believe in the good news'" (Mark 1:14-15). This proclamation indicates a point of time in salvation history on which various factors converge: iniquity has reached its full measure (Matt. 23:32) and calls for the fulfillment of the prophecies of salvation (Matt. 13:17) for both Jews and Gentiles (Luke 2:32; 24:47). It is a change of era, the inauguration of the period of grace in preparation for the end. "Repent" does not mean simply sorrow for one's sins; *metanoia* is a complete change of mentality, a new *Weltanschauung* in the light of God's present initiative; even the Pharisees who fasted, prayed, and observed the law needed *metanoia*. "Belief in the gospel" is the unconditional acceptance of Jesus' proclamation to participate in the new spiritual and cosmic order inaugurated by him, which will reach its perfection in his second coming to make everything new. It is this complete confidence and trust that allows miracles to take place; without them, even Jesus' authority is impotent. "Your faith has made you whole" and similar praises occur often (Mark 5:34; 10:52; Luke 8:48;

Matt. 9:29). Assent to the gospel includes reception of Jesus himself, not only as its announcer, for also John had proclaimed its coming, but as the person through whom the power of the Father's sovereignty operates.

The response to God's grace is proportionate to its progressive endowment. Jesus' moral requirements are so much higher than those of Moses and the prophets as is the intensity of the Father's favor in the inauguration of the kingdom, whose power will render possible such a response.

The Urgency of the Decision

The "Yes" to Jesus' call is urgent; it allows for no doubt or procrastination. This is illustrated by many parables and sayings. A man who decided to follow Jesus but wanted to wait until he could bury his father, and another who asked to take leave of his family before becoming a disciple are not allowed any respite (Luke 9:59-62). This is equivalent to hating — in the Semitic sense of loving less — father, mother, and brothers in favor of the supreme value of following Jesus (Luke 14:26). Obstacles to this decision may be as dear to us as our right eye or right hand; if so, then these too the true disciple must sacrifice (Matt. 18:9). According to some interpretations of Matthew 11:12ff., fellowship requires violence over oneself to be faultless. This serious decision is not required only from those who enter the kingdom, but should be extended at all times to all initiatives taken within the kingdom like marriage, profession of vows, and dedication to mission and ministry.

The urgency of this existential decision is expressed in those parables sometimes called the "parables of crisis"; they describe someone who has been caught up in critical and threatening circumstances and must make a choice immediately if he wants to save himself from disaster. Such a one is the crafty steward who had misappropriated his master's goods and has now been caught red-handed. It is precisely his craftiness that saves him; he will endear his creditors by following Macbeth's maxim that "things bad begun make strong themselves by ill" and detract a proportion of what they owe so that they may show him kindness when he is dismissed (Luke 16:1-9). Jesus praises him not for his dishonesty or for his embezzlements but for the immediacy of his astute decision. It is a situation identical with that of a rich sinner, caught unawares by threat of judgment, who immediately distributes his superfluous wealth to the poor to gain their intercession. Likewise, a general in command of ten thousand men finds himself faced by an army of twenty thousand. He must decide immediately whether to engage in battle or beg for a truce; the safety of his army and his own honor depend on his choice (Luke 14:31-33).

The joy one has on hearing the gospel message about the coming kingdom is similar to that of a man who has discovered a treasure buried in a field. He will sell all his goods to be able to buy that field (Matt. 13:44). These parables are often addressed to the wealthy, those who have to choose between their dear possessions and the much greater treasure offered in the kingdom.

What distinguishes between the various reactions to Jesus' call? The parable of the seed that falls on different kinds on ground — barren, rocky, thorny, or fertile — illustrates this. Such are humans' hearts: hardened, weak, superficial, or responsive to varying degrees (Mark 4:2-20).

Love Requires Love

It is often said that the God of the New Testament is a God of love and mercy while the Old Testament Deity is the severe, punishing judge. Nothing can be more false. As we saw, the main themes of the psalms are mercy, forgiveness, and love. Some passages in

Ezekiel are particularly moving, especially chapter 16 about Israel as the unfaithful bride of Yahweh who has betrayed him with all false gods; in spite of her infidelity, God takes her back and loves her again. On the other hand we find fearful "woes" in the New Testament, against the rich in Luke 6:24 and against the Pharisees in Matthew 23. Threats of judgment are to be found in the Gospels, not to speak about the visions of the Apocalypse. Marcion's separation of the good New Testament god and the just Old Testament god, as also the Gnostic distinction between the supreme unknowable Father and the demiurge creator of the world, have always been rejected by the church as unfaithful to both Testaments and to church tradition.

Jesus' death is never presented in the New Testament as a self-immolation to placate the Father's wrath. Both Paul and John assert that the saving initiative came from God himself in spite of humanity's unworthiness (Rom. 5:1-10; 1 John 4:7-12); hence the response to love is love: of both God and neighbor. The Ten Commandments showed Israel the way to show gratitude for God's liberation from bondage and for her election. In his answer to the enquiring and sincere scribe Jesus sums up the precepts in the first commandment: "'Hear, O Israel: The Lord our God, the Lord is one; you shall love the Lord your God with all your heart, and with all your soul, and with all your mind, and with all your strength.' The second is this, 'You shall love your neighbor as yourself.' There is no other commandment greater than these" (Mark 12:29-31; Deut. 6:5; Lev. 19:18). As Jesus had asserted that he had come not to abolish the law but to fulfill and perfect it (Matt. 5:17), his teaching can be considered as the way to put these precepts into practice in the context of the advent of the kingdom, especially as regards the meaning of "neighbor."

At this point it is appropriate to ask: what does loving an invisible and transcendent God mean? John gives a practical answer when he asserts, "No one has ever seen God. It is God the only Son, who is close to the Father's heart, who has made him known" (John 1:18). Hence: "Whoever has seen me has seen the Father" (John 14:9); "Those who love me will keep my word, and my Father will love him, and we will come to them and make our home with them" (14:23). Therefore, as Jesus is the visible sign of the kingdom he is God made visible, and hence lovable. The observance of Christ's commandments is the practical way to love both him and the Father. The Synoptic parallel to these Johannine sayings is Matthew 11:27: "All things have been handed over to me by my Father; and no one knows the Son except the Father, and no one knows the Father except the Son and anyone to whom the Son chooses to reveal him."

We can go even further: if love is the harmony of wills and of affections, we love God when we make his interests our own, and moreover, render them the main purpose of our existence. As already hinted above, the Father's interests are spelled out in the first three petitions of the Our Father: the hallowing of his name, the coming of his kingdom, and the fulfillment of his will. We turn to the meaning of these prayer-programs later on.

Jesus' teaching goes far beyond the Old Testament where love of neighbor is concerned. We certainly do find edifying examples of behavior and benevolent codes of conduct in the old dispensation. David's comportment with his persecutor Saul in 1 Samuel 26 and his mourning over the death of this king in 2 Samuel 1 are meant to be paradigmatic; so are the prescriptions of the Israelite's behavior towards alien inhabitants, widows, and orphans in Deuteronomy 24:17-21. The attitude of many psalms towards one's enemies, however, falls way behind Jesus' redefinition of "neighbor" in the Gospels. He is no longer the Jewish brother or the alien; the parable of the Good Samaritan in Luke 10:25-37 extends the term to cover any other human being, friend or foe, who is in need of your help in any particular circumstance. The reason is that we have one Father who is in heaven and therefore we are all brothers and sisters (Matt. 23:9); "he makes his sun rise on the evil and on the good, and sends rain on the righteous and on the unrighteous" (Matt. 5:45); he gives freely and expects us to do the same (Matt. 10:8). "Be perfect, therefore, as your heavenly Father is perfect" (Matt. 5:48). Clearly a premise that posits an unreachable ideal has far-reaching consequences. The Good Samaritan helped a racial enemy whom he considered as his neighbor, but had this enemy been aggressive, what would have been his reaction? Would hatred have been justified? Jesus is not satisfied by mere non-hatred: he requires positive love and prayer for persecutors (Matt. 5:43-44). Nor is it sufficient to abstain from doing to others what we would not like to be done to us, a maxim that we find in other religions. The gospel calls for the kind of positive help that we would wish to receive ourselves (Matt. 7:12). And if this is not sufficient to define the word "neighbor," Jesus adds the marginalized and outcasts to the list who are to be preferred to well-to-do colleagues: "When you give a banquet, invite the poor, the crippled, the lame, and the blind. And you will be blessed, because they cannot repay you, for you will be repaid at the resurrection of the righteous" (Luke 14:13-14).

The principle of being perfect as your heavenly Father is perfect requires the forgiveness of enemies and of any wrongdoing. The kingdom in its aspect of an amnesty offered to a humanity alienated from God, open to embrace anyone who repents, traces a pattern for all those who accept the words of Jesus to follow him. The relationship between prior forgiveness and mutual pardoning is well illustrated in the parable of the king who cancelled the huge debt of a thousand talents of one of his servants who could not ever hope to repay it and the behavior of this same servant towards his fellow steward, strangling him to give back the comparatively petty sum of a hundred denarii (Matt. 18:23-35). The parable illustrates the disproportion between inter-human wrongs and offenses and the debt incurred by sin towards God. The Matthean version of the fifth petition of the Our Father, "Forgive us our debts, as we also have forgiven our debtors" (6:12), now reverses the process of prior forgiveness and makes it an unconditional requirement for the acceptance of our prayers and sacrifices: "So when you are offering your gift at the altar, if you remember that your brother or sister has something against you, leave your gift there before the altar and go; first be reconciled to your brother or sister, and then come and offer your gift" (Matt. 5:23-24). The saying refers to Old Testament sacrifices; it becomes even more severe if we apply it to the Eucharistic sacrifice.

The Kingdom versus Mammon

It is clear that Jesus' requirements rub against the grain of human nature. If they are to make sense in anyone's life they call for a complete revolution in the current scale of values: "For what will it profit them if they gain the whole world but forfeit their life? Or what will they give in return for their life?" (Matt. 16:26). The Beatitudes that open the Sermon on the Mount are definitely absurd in the eyes of ordinary society; happiness belongs to the rich, the powerful, to those who have a good time often at the expense of the weak. Their bliss, as long as it lasts, belongs to this world, but the parameters of the kingdom extend far beyond human estimates, and the measure of happiness is to be assessed in relation to this broader perspective. In this view real happiness belongs to the poor, to those who mourn, to the meek, the hungry, the merciful, the pure in heart, the peacemakers, and the persecuted. Some philosophers and religious sages had already glimpsed this truth in a psychological or social context; now in the frame of reference of Jesus' preaching the Beatitudes acquire an eschatological connotation.

Who are the poor and what is the nature of the reward that is able to transform their sorrow into joy? It is well known that there are two versions of the Beatitudes, the Lukan and the Matthean. The former (Luke 6:20-26) contains four beatitudes and four woes, opposing the poor and the rich, the hungry and those who are full, those who weep and those who now laugh, and the persecuted and the well-spoken-of. The categories are social, implying marginalization. Matthew 5:3-12 has eight beatitudes without the corresponding woes, which tend towards spiritualization: the poor are the "poor in spirit" and the hungry are those who hunger and thirst for righteousness. It is obvious that not all the economically poor are righteous or pious. The interpretation of these categories is to be found in the Old Testament. Psalm 49 contains a good description of the attitudes of the rich: they "trust in their wealth and boast of the abundance of their riches" (v. 6); their wealth will not descend with them into the grave; "though in their lifetime they count themselves happy" because they are praised by all, they "will never again see the light" (vv. 17-19); their wealth and pomp cannot ransom them (v. 7). The poor man, on the contrary, has no one to turn to but God. He is kicked around by the mighty and suffers injustice, he has no say in society, but his richness consists in his trust in God who will ultimately deliver and avenge him (Ps. 52). In fact, the eight beatitudes are almost all variations on the theme "poor" as described in these psalms. In Jesus' time "the poor of Yahweh" formed a category of their own, to which such people as Mary belonged. The Magnificat is an expression of their piety. They were not destitute; they belonged to what we may call a lower-middle class, but their poverty was qualified by their meekness, their mercy, and their spiritual stance. The Bible does not canonize misery; in fact it works toward abolishing it through social justice and almsgiving. There is an economic level below which one cannot live as a human being, and an upper level above which one cannot live as a believer unless one shares with the destitute. The poor, therefore, are those who, according to their status in life, are bracketed in between, defined by their humility and their faith.

The promises to the poor are couched in the future and reveal various facets of the kingdom: mourners will be comforted; the meek shall inherit the land (see Ps. 37:11; that is, will enjoy peace and abundance after their strenuous march through life); the hunger for righteousness will be satisfied; the merciful will be repaid with mercy; the pure in heart, that is, sincere people without any duplicity, shall behold God, who can only be perceived with a simple heart; and peacemakers will be called children of God, who is a God of peace. The fulfillment of these promises is not entirely eschatological in the sense of ultra-terrestrial. The kingdom is both present and future, both spiritual and social, so the poor will leave it to God to decide when and how he will meet their yearnings. When Peter voices the desire of the disciples to know what recompense they will have for having left all to follow Jesus, the answer is that they will receive "a hundredfold now in this age — houses, brothers and sisters, mothers and children, and fields with persecutions — and in the age to come eternal life" (Mark 10:30).

The great obstacle to entry into the kingdom is mammon, that is, riches, *pleonexia*, the heaping up of worldly goods. Before trying to understand why God and mammon are not reconcilable we must circumscribe the meaning of this word in its historical social setting. Today we in the West measure richness or poverty mostly by means of income. Industrialists and financiers are a class of their own whom we consider the richest. Taxes are usually used for social purposes: pensions, hospitals, social services, and so forth. In the biblical world immense wealth was accumulated in the hands of a few privileged families who manifested their splendor by means of the number of their retainers, of *patronatus*, prodigal feasting, and endowment of public works. The poor could only rely on almsgiving and some casual work for their sustenance. This is a generalization, of course, but it provides a background for understanding Jesus' stance on the perils of superfluous wealth, often ill-gotten. The difference between social conditions then and now does not obliterate the fact of poverty and misery in our own days on the individual, class, and international levels, so the New Testament emphasis on the distribution of wealth is still pertinent. What Jesus says about rich individuals applies to the wealthier strata of society and to the "first world" nations that often thrive on the poorer countries' weak economies, so that the rich become ever richer and the poor fall into misery, according to this oft-repeated phrase. We also know — alas! — that financial help from the richer countries can run aground within indigent societies if it remains in the hands of the governing few, thus reiterating the whole process.

The parable of the rich man and Lazarus in Luke 16:19-31 portrays well the *doxa*, the pomp and social splendor of the rich as described above, and the contrast between superfluous magnificence and misery in this world and its inversion in the next. At the root of the rich man's disdain is his self-centeredness, his lack of feeling towards the needs of others, but mostly the sense of power and self-sufficiency provoked by the adulation of his social clients. He has no need for God and is oblivious of the precariousness of his existence: "And God said to him, 'You fool! This very night your life is being demanded of you. And the things you have prepared, whose will they be?' So it is for those who store up treasures for themselves but are not rich toward God" (Luke 12:20-21). The role of the two characters in the parable is reversed: the rich man is now the beggar, and Lazarus receives the reward of the eschatological kingdom promised in the first beatitude.

The only way for a rich person to inherit eternal life is that which Jesus proposes to the wealthy man who ran up to him asking him what he should do to be saved (Mark 10:17-22). The answer: first of all observe the commandments. This is essential to be loved by Christ, but to follow him it is not enough: "'You lack one thing;

go, sell what you own, and give the money to the poor, and you will have treasure in heaven; then come, follow me.' When he heard this, he was shocked and went away grieving, for he had many possessions." After this encounter Jesus adds: "It is easier for a camel to go through the eye of a needle than for someone who is rich to enter the kingdom of God." This discourages even the disciples themselves, who ask him, who then can ever be saved? Jesus is well aware that he is asking for an effort that surpasses human possibilities, and adds: "For mortals it is impossible, but not for God; for God all things are possible" (Mark 10:23-27). Paul will unfold the full import of this saying in his theology of the Spirit who overcomes the weakness of the "flesh," of human frailty.

A saying in Luke enters more deeply into the human heart: "Sell your possessions, and give alms. Make purses for yourselves that do not wear out, an unfailing treasure in heaven, where no thief comes near and no moth destroys. For where your treasure is, there your heart will be also" (Luke 12:33-34), which brings us back to the kingdom as a supreme value and the orientation of all desires, thoughts, loves, and deeds towards it. If accumulation of wealth becomes the prime goal of life it will invariably draw all the activities of the human psyche towards itself. This principle does not apply only to riches but to any other value incompatible with the demands of the kingdom.

Jesus considers hoarding riches as a lack of faith. A word that often recurs in the Gospels is "anxiety." We speak today of "anxiety neurosis" — the will to build one's own future with one's own hands, riding roughshod on the rights of others, and leaving nothing to God's care for us. The beautiful passage in Matthew 6:25-34 about the birds of the air and the lilies of the field is an invitation to stop worrying overmuch about material things and to place our trust in God's love and providence: "Strive first for the kingdom of God and his righteousness, and all these things will be given to you as well. So do not worry about tomorrow, for tomorrow will bring worries of its own. Today's trouble is enough for today" (vv. 33-34).

Almsgiving can become a cold, habitual process, or even a means of ostentation if it does not spring from a deep feeling of mercy. The merciful are called blessed in the beatitudes, and they shall receive back what they now give (Matt. 5:7). Mercy is the sacrifice of the heart, nobler than the temple sacrifices (Matt. 9:13). What we usually call "mercy" is only a partial translation of the Hebrew *hesed,* which includes faithfulness, loyalty, grace, and kindness, especially when referring to the relationship between God and humanity, God and the people of the covenant, thus becoming the model of inter-human relationships. As such it becomes the very soul of prayer. The parables on mutual forgiveness cited earlier in this chapter define mercy as passing on to our neighbor what we, both as humankind and as individuals, have received from God. Portia in *The Merchant of Venice* (IV:i) summarizes very well the gospel message when she says that mercy "droppeth as the gentle rain from heaven/Upon the place beneath. It is twice blest:/It blesseth him that gives and him that takes."

Poverty as Humility

As we have seen, "poor in spirit" in Matthew has a broader sense than the socially poor as opposed to the rich in Luke; there is an even deeper understanding of the word, however, if we place it in the context of Jesus' continual controversies with the Pharisees. This term needs some explanation, as it has been the source of regretful misunderstanding. The Pharisaic movement had its origin in the second century BCE when life became very difficult for those who wanted to live according to the law of Moses. This group of people vowed to observe the law to its last detail, and, to make sure that they would not even approach the material transgression of any precept, they added traditions of their own, which they attributed to an oral tradition handed down by Moses, thus building, as they put it, "a hedge around the law," that would keep them far from legal offense. These traditions were mainly concerned with the categories "pure" and "impure" as applied to foods, states of life, and actions. There is no doubt that their intentions were laudable. Psychologically and spiritually speaking, however, Pharisaism was not devoid of dangers. First of all, the categories "pure" and "impure" sometimes substituted "moral" and "immoral"; people would be content with the material observance of certain prescriptions and forget the inner spirit or purpose of the commandments; people employed endless casuistry to disentangle themselves from legal obligations; the tendency to "count merits" and balance them against demerits led to a mathematical spirituality; people tended to look down on the ignorant as impure; and lastly, the person who felt so pure and full of credit was inclined to consider God as his creditor. Understood this way, people conceived religion as giving something to God instead of it as expressing gratitude for the gift of righteousness. Essentially they reduced grace to barter.

Pharisaic attitudes, at least as they are portrayed in the Gospels, are not limited to members of the sect in Jesus' time. The Pharisees later gained the upper hand in the conflict between the various tendencies of Judaism after the year 70. Such attitudes are deeply rooted in any religion and in any society monitored by laws. Within the historical sect itself there were numberless sincere and pious people who suffered for their faithfulness to the law, and we must not forget that many of the first Christians were indeed Pharisees, including Paul himself. It was, however, precisely some pristine followers of this sect who, like the elder brother in the parable of the prodigal son, opposed the entry of the Gentiles into the church without the requirement of circumcision and law-observance. Within the church, medieval piety sometimes degenerated into an enumeration of indulgences, which provoked Luther's reaction. Even today that temptation is inevitable and Jesus' parables and controversies are still valid for both Christians and non-Christians alike because there can also be a "lay Pharisaism" deep in the heart of non-believers as well: the "holier-than-thou" attitude works both ways.

Now the gospel of the kingdom announced by Jesus was an offer of unmerited grace for sinners, God's free gift, to which the greatest obstacle would be a feeling of self-sufficiency and self-righteousness. This explains the resistance of the scribes and Pharisees and must be kept in mind when we come to Paul's doctrine of justification.

Within this context many of Jesus' sayings and parables fall into place. An example is the caricature of the Pharisee in Luke 18:9-14 who went up to the temple and praised God because he was not like other men, sinners, extortionists, adulterers, or like that publican over there. Though he paid his tithes and fasted twice a week he had certainly not heard Jesus' word: "When you have done all that you were ordered to do, say, 'We are worthless slaves; we have done only what we ought to have done!'" (Luke 17:10), which illustrates well the perils of Pharisaism. This man came up to praise himself rather than God; what did he expect? Should God have come down to thank him? Religion does not consist of giving something to God but is simply the acknowledgment that all we possess, including our piety, is a gift. The tax collector of the parable is justified because he simply admits his moral bankruptcy and asks for gratuitous forgiveness. So did the criminal crucified with Jesus (Luke 23:42-43).

The parable of the prodigal son, with its emphasis on the elder brother's refusal to participate in the father's rejoicing, also reflects the stance of the Pharisees with regard to Jesus' acceptance of sinners, and will later manifest itself in the primitive church that is prepared to accept Gentile converts without the requirement of circumcision and legal observances. The narrative implies that in spite of the dutiful nearness to the Father of the "just," they often fail to penetrate into the Father's loving nature owing to their juridical concept of piety, while the sinner's sense of existential emptiness echoes the distant voice of a Father who is prepared not only to forgive but also to embrace and reinstate.

Although the priest and the Levite who passed by the stricken man in the parable of the Good Samaritan (Luke 10:30-37) may not have been Pharisees, they must have certainly experienced a conflict between their human instinct of pity and the retention of their state of legal purity by not touching blood, while the Samaritan had no such hesitation. This is another instance of how a legalistic approach to religion may suffocate the nobler inclinations of the heart and the observance of the more essential moral precepts, which is rendered more explicit by Jesus' severe tirade of woes against the insincere casuistry of rabbinic legalism in Matthew 23:13-36. It is obvious that legalistic hypocrisy is not limited to midrashic interpretation, which can cite numerous instances of deep spirituality, but is a prerogative of casuistry, whether it is to be found among civil legalists or canon lawyers. It is the effort to extricate one from moral obligations by means of quibbling rationalizations.

If laws are a source of hypocrisy are they therefore to be abolished? This is absurd; no society can exist without some form of legislation, and Jesus is clear about his relation to the Mosaic law. He insists on the observance of the commandments (Matt. 15:3, 6; 19:17), but new wine must be poured into new wineskins; patching up old garments ruins both dress and patch (Mark 2:21-22). Jesus has not come to abolish but to fulfill the law. The verb *pleroo* used in Matthew 5:17, in its Jewish meaning, means the fulfilling of prophecy, but as "law" it includes the whole of the Old Testament. It also means observance, but, as the subsequent six antitheses indicate, Jesus perfects both the legislation and its interpretation by updating it and inserting it into the new context of the kingdom. We said above that the Pharisees intended to build a hedge around the law to prevent its transgression; this they did by adding precept upon precept from a tradition that they claimed derived orally from Moses himself. Jesus too has a similar intention, but he does not multiply commandments; he simply descends more deeply into the root intent of the commandments as such and into the innermost motivations of the heart. He knows that if these are purified there is no danger of external transgression. Thus by avoiding getting angry with someone a person will not arrive at the point of killing; by not looking lecherously at a woman one will avoid adultery; to avoid perjury do not swear at all but speak with sincerity (Matt. 5:21-48).

Many laws concerning ritual purity and impurity centered on the sacrificial cult in the temple. An "impure" man or woman could not take part unless he or she went through the ritual purifications. Pure and impure were categories different from moral and immoral; some things that rendered a person impure were eminently moral, such as childbirth or preparing the dead for burial. Jesus' famous saying, "Destroy this temple, and in three days I will raise it up" (John 2:19), which according to Mark 14:58 occasioned his condemnation, reveals his consciousness of the coming shift of the cult from the temple to the new community he was gathering around him. In fact he claims to be greater than the temple itself (Matt. 12:6) and to be lord of the sabbath (Mark 2:28). The new temple will not be governed by the laws of purity but by faith in Jesus and by the single commandment of love of God and neighbor.

The conclusions that the early Christians drew from these premises are scattered throughout the rest of the New Testament. John clarifies that Jesus was speaking of the temple of his own body (2:19-22), which rose again on the third day. Paul calls the church the body of Christ as well as the temple of God (Rom. 12:4-5; 1 Cor. 12:12-14; see Eph. 1:23). The main theme of the Epistle to the Hebrews is that Christ is the only priest of the new dispensation and his blood the only sacrifice. "For when there is a change in the priesthood, there is necessarily a change in the law as well" (Heb. 7:12). Christians participate in this sacrifice in the celebration of the Eucharist (1 Cor. 10:16-17; 11:26). Hence the new worship of the Father "in spirit and truth," not in Jerusalem, nor in Samaria (John 4:23ff.), has been inaugurated by the resurrection of Christ. The old cultic laws and the categories of pure and impure are therefore obsolete; there is only one state of purity, the moral purity required by Jesus and generated in the believer by the "law of the Spirit" (Rom. 8:2). Worship is now *eucharistia*, thanksgiving, the expression of gratitude to the Father of our Lord Jesus Christ, "who has blessed us in Christ with every spiritual blessing in the heavenly places . . . as a plan for the fullness of time, to gather up all things in him, things in heaven and things on earth" (Eph. 1:3, 10). It is precisely the "new wine" referred to in Mark 2:22.

This excursus into the New Testament writings outside of the Synoptics was necessary as an example of how the early church rendered explicit Jesus' sayings and to show the difference between a cultic spirituality based on rabbinic reasoning and one based on the revelation of the inauguration of the kingdom. The two are not in opposition to one another; there is continuity, for the old sacrificial system, too, was God's revelation, a type that prefaced the unimaginable leap into the reality of the new worship (Heb. 8:5), itself but a shadow of the eschatological heavenly worship.

Knowing the Father and Knowing Christ

Euangelion, gospel, means the announcement of good news, the news that the erstwhile foretold inauguration of God's sovereignty is now taking place. Jesus was no mere proclaimer of the kingdom as was John the Baptist who had announced it before him (Matt. 3:2). His presence and his sending were the core of the kingdom;

there could be no reception of the kingdom without acknowledging Jesus as the promised Christ. Such an act of faith would need the same spiritual dispositions and would encounter the same obstacles as did the kingdom. The confession of Jesus as the Christ, however, called for something more. We have two apparently conflicting texts in the Synoptics that require a reference to John to make sense. In fact, the first saying, Matthew 11:27, is often called the lightning-flash from the Johannine sky: "All things have been handed over to me by my Father; and no one knows the Son except the Father, and no one knows the Father except the Son and anyone to whom the Son chooses to reveal him." Knowing in the biblical sense is not merely intellectual comprehension, but a mutual and intimate relationship between persons, and Jesus proclaims as exclusive his relationship with the Father. The Father is unknowable: "No one has ever seen God. It is God the only Son, who is close to the Father's heart, who has made him known" (John 1:18). This implies that not even Moses or Isaiah beheld the true face of God; the Son alone "knows" him and he alone can grant the psalmist's cry: "Restore us, O God; let your face shine, that we may be saved" (Ps. 80:3; also vv. 7 and 19). He is the true countenance of the Father, and it is in his power to reveal him to whomsoever he wills. On the other hand, when Peter confesses that Jesus is the Christ, the Son of God, Jesus replies: "Blessed are you, Simon son of Jonah! For flesh and blood has not revealed this to you, but my Father in heaven" (Matt. 16:17). "Flesh and blood" means human nature, rational understanding. Faith is something to which reason cannot give birth, for it is a supernatural gift. We may justifiably ask, however, whether it is the Son who reveals the Father or the Father who reveals the Son. It is here that John can provide a suitable answer; the vicious circle cannot be resolved unless we introduce a third factor, the Spirit: "When the Advocate comes, whom I will send to you from the Father, the Spirit of truth who comes from the Father, he will testify on my behalf. You also are to testify because you have been with me from the beginning" (John 15:26-27). Therefore the Father sends his Spirit to the believer, this same Spirit reveals Jesus as the Christ, the Son of God, and Christ then reveals the Father; it is this same Spirit that will endow the disciples with fortitude to confess Christ before tribunals (Mark 13:9-11).

The obstacles and the required dispositions to accept Jesus as the Messiah are the same as those that admit into or exclude from the kingdom. Jesus was rejected by the majority of the scribes, the Pharisees, and the priests; by his own countrymen in Nazareth because his claims were not commensurate with his lowly family; and by the rich man who was loath to relinquish his wealth; but he was hailed by repentant publicans and sinners, and especially by children and those with a childlike spirit.

Acknowledging and confessing Jesus as the Christ is not enough. He must be accepted as the suffering and crucified Messiah. Peter was praised for having professed him as the Christ, but was immediately reprehended when he showed his revulsion at Jesus' prophecy that "he must go to Jerusalem and undergo great suffering at the hands of the elders and chief priests and scribes, and be killed" (Matt. 16:21). The disciple of the Crucified One will himself carry Jesus' cross: "If any want to become my followers, let them deny themselves and take up their cross and follow me. For those who want to save their life will lose it, and those who lose their life for my sake will find it" (Matt. 16:24-25). Carrying the cross does not only mean suffering for the sake of one's discipleship, but also implies living the whole gospel of Jesus. Luke implies this by incorporating so many of Jesus' most well-known sayings into the journey towards Jerusalem (9:51–19:27), which means that discipleship entails following Jesus' teaching with humble obedience on his way to Calvary to be able to rise again with him.

There is an "Adamic" suffering which is common to all men: sickness and various afflictions, natural disasters and emotional pain; but there are other sufferings which are inherent in the kingdom, and especially in Christian discipleship. They need not lead to martyrdom but they do belong to the personal hardships and inconveniences of living up to gospel standards, as well as being looked down upon socially in societies which consider Christian integrity absurd and ridiculous.

Imitation and Witness

Jesus nonetheless encourages us to take up his yoke: "Come to me, all you that are weary and are carrying heavy burdens, and I will give you rest. Take my yoke upon you, and learn from me; for I am gentle and humble in heart, and you will find rest for your souls. For my yoke is easy, and my burden is light" (Matt. 11:28-30). The rabbis spoke about the yoke of the law, with its 613 precepts and declared it light. The new law, the "law of the Spirit of life in Christ Jesus," as Paul calls it (Rom. 8:2), the Spirit of freedom (2 Cor. 3:17), is embodied in Christ, who, in spite of the radical demands of the gospel, helps his followers to carry this yoke with joy and freedom, because he does for them what Simon of Cyrene will later do for him. The invitation to imitate him is the only one we find in the Gospels; he is meek because he is an object of disdain, but humble of heart because his only trust is in the Father. The promised rest is certainly not the absence of hardships and adversities — the Christian life is after all a continuous struggle — but that internal peace of heart begotten by love and experienced by those who are confident that they are walking along the right path towards a secure goal. Jesus' behest to be perfect as our heavenly Father is perfect in Matthew 5:48 certainly posits an unreachable ideal, for it is only he, who knows the Father as he is known by the Father, who attains that perfection; yet following him means treading the path towards that ideal.

The joy engendered by the decision of faith and by the confession of Jesus as the Christ the Son of God cannot be kept for oneself alone. It needs to be shared with others through witness and mission: "You are the salt of the earth. . . . You are the light of the world. A city built on a hill cannot be hid. No one after lighting a lamp puts it under the bushel basket, but on the lampstand, and it gives light to all in the house. In the same way, let your light shine before others, so that they may see your good works and give glory to your Father in heaven" (Matt. 5:13-16). Therefore we give witness by our actions that flow naturally from the change of personality brought about by believing. Good works should not draw attention to our supposed holiness, as the saying about the practice of virtue to be seen by others warns: "Beware of practicing your piety before others in order to be seen by them; for then you have no reward from your Father in heaven" (Matt. 6:1-6). Praise should pass through us without touching us and rise immediately to the Father to whom we owe even our good works. On the other hand, hiding the lamp under a bushel basket points to being ashamed of one's faith: "I tell you, every one who acknowledges me before others, the Son of Man also will acknowledge before the angels of God; but whoever denies me before others will be denied before the angels of God" (Luke 12:8-9).

During his public ministry Jesus sent the twelve to preach the kingdom and to heal. The efficacy of their mission did not depend on their material means but on the power with which he endowed them (Luke 9:1-6). "You received without payment; give without payment" (Matt. 10:8). After sending the twelve he broadens the assignment by sending seventy disciples with the same instructions "ahead of him in pairs to every town and place where he himself intended to go" (Luke 10:1). The seventy disciples represent that missionary activity, which is not limited to the apostles but is to be carried out by all believers. As it takes two to bear testimony, they are sent in pairs so that their witness may be valid. Christ will follow their preaching with his own presence. They are even exhorted to pray for more workers in this field (Luke 10:2). After his resurrection Jesus again broadens the mission of the apostles, showing that it will not be confined to Israel and to the Jews: "All authority in heaven and on earth has been given to me. Go therefore and make disciples of all nations, baptizing them in the name of the Father and of the Son and of the Holy Spirit, and teaching them to obey everything that I have commanded you. And remember, I am with you always, to the end of the age" (Matt. 28:18-20). The book of Acts describes this preaching, but the spread of Christianity in the first centuries is the merit of simple Christians, travelers, slaves, husbands and wives, merchants and scholars who were eager to share their experience with others in their company. The presence of Christ himself followed in the faith of all those who received his word through their witness.

Mission may lead to persecution; the long discourse that follows the sending of the twelve (Matt. 10:16-42) forewarns the apostles of their fate, so that they may not be dismayed and discouraged when they encounter difficulties; the kingdom itself suffers violence (Matt. 11:12), and so do those who preach it. The predictions are very specific; for Matthew's community they already form part of their experience.

The disciples will be like sheep among wolves. To survive they must combine craftiness and innocence (Matt. 10:16), not an easy task at all. They will be dragged before all kinds of tribunals, from synagogues to imperial courts, and flogged. Let them not worry about what they will say, for the Holy Spirit will inspire them (vv. 17-20). Early Christians collected these testimonies in the Acts of the Martyrs and commented on them as prophetical sayings. Moreover, believers will be accused of being Christian by members of their own family and will be often compelled to flee to another city (vv. 21-23). In fact, Jesus reminds them, "Do not think that I have come to bring peace to the earth; I have not come to bring peace, but a sword" (v. 34). Being servants of Jesus, they cannot escape his own fate; men can destroy their bodies, but not their souls. Despite these afflictions, they must persevere in their preaching because the Father will keep a vigilant eye on them and truth will prevail in the end (vv. 26-31). We must not read these sayings as referring only to early Christianity; a survey of the history of the church and a mere look around us in our own times will suffice to put us on our guard even today. On the other hand, it is necessary to keep in mind that in times past when Christians had the upper hand they did to others what they now complain is being done to them.

In these circumstances the parables that exhort to vigilance are still very actual and can be summed up in Jesus' admonition: "Keep awake and pray that you may not come into the time of trial; the spirit indeed is willing, but the flesh is weak (Mark 14:38). This leads us to the important subject of prayer.

Prayer

Jesus and his family were pious Jews, frequenting both the temple and the synagogue; their prayers included the *berakhu*, the recitation of the Decalogue, the *shema*, the *amidah* or blessings, the *aleynu* and the *kaddish* as well as the *hevdolah* before the sabbath meal, in whatever form these prayers were recited in the beginning of the first century. Yet we read that Jesus often prayed alone (Mark 1:35), that he went up to a mountain to pray (Mark 6:46), that he prayed after his baptism by John (Luke 3:21), at his transfiguration (Luke 9:29), that before his passion he prayed for Peter's faith, and that he prayed in the garden of Gethsemane (Mark 14:35-39). Except in the last two instances we do not know anything about the content of these prayers. We certainly have the long "priestly prayer" in John 17, but how much of it is Johannine redaction is not certain.

Prayer is essentially communion of the mind with God in

which we both express praise, thanksgiving, and petition, and at the same time receive new insights into the mystery of salvation. It is the Holy Spirit who prompts our spirit to ask for what is most necessary (cf. Rom. 8:26-27). Christ's prayer can only be imagined as reaching the peak of intensity in such a communion.

Apart from the Our Father, which we shall examine later, Jesus rarely instructs his disciples on the object of their petition. He exhorts them to ask the Father to send workers into the harvest (Matt. 9:38), that their flight in the days of tribulation may not occur in winter or on a sabbath (Matt. 24:20) and, in Gethsemane, that they not fall into temptation (Mark 14:38). Yet though he rarely determines their petition, he does insist on how to pray.

In his Sermon on the Mount Jesus warns against performing the three acts of piety — fasting, prayer, and almsgiving — to be seen and praised by others (Matt. 6:1-15). The hypocrites pray showing off in public; if it is approval they are seeking, they do receive it, but not from God. The parable of the Pharisee and the tax collector illustrates this saying well (Luke 18:10-14). Prayer should take place in the innermost chambers of the heart so that it may be appreciated and granted only by God (Matt. 6:6). Gentiles, on the other hand, heap up words on words, thinking that the longer the prayer the better the chances of being heard by the gods. Jesus summarizes the essence of prayer in the Our Father.

Faith is the primary condition to render prayer effective. Jesus often praises the faith of those who ask for healing, for no prayer will go lost in the hands of a merciful and omnipotent Father. We should, he says, precede our petition for forgiveness by forgiving our own debtors (Mark 11:25). Belief shows itself in perseverance (Luke 11:5-8; 18:1-8; 21:36), as the parables of the petitioner at midnight and the reluctant judge demonstrate. These parables are an *a fortiori* argument to convince those who pray that if among humans even importune repeated petition will obtain its request from people who do not want to be bothered, much more so does the good God respond to persevering petitions. The Father will certainly grant what we ask for, but he will not give us "a snake instead of a fish" or a scorpion instead of an egg (Luke 11:11-12); instead he will grant the Holy Spirit, who is the essential gift of God. This may be a warning not to ask for harmful or unnecessary things, which we often do in prayer, but for the essentials of God's kingdom. What these essentials are Jesus lists in the Our Father.

The Our Father reflects phrases of Jewish prayers, especially the *amidah* and the *kaddish*, which Jesus recited from his childhood. Its originality lies in the selection Jesus made of essential petitions and their insertion into the context of the coming of God's Kingship. It is not merely "a prayer" to be recited but rather a formulary of prayers, each of which can be taken apart and expanded on, like variations on a theme, in loving meditation. In his letter 130, St. Augustine explains the Lord's Prayer and says that we can only ask with the certainty of receiving whatever is contained in the Our Father; anything extraneous we petition is not sure to be granted. He sees the Lord's Prayer as the summary of the whole Psalter, for each one of the one hundred fifty psalms can be categorized within the seven petitions of this prayer. Each petition of the prayer asks something from the Father but at the same time challenges the petitioner not only to cooperate in its realization but also to make it a goal of his existence, that is, to dedicate his life to the glorification of God, to work for his kingdom, to do his will, to share his bread with the poor, to forgive, to combat temptation and evil. The main actor is always the Father, however, who requires a response in thought, word, and deed.

The prayer is divided into three sections: after the invocation, "Our Father who art in heaven," the first three petitions ask something for God himself; the other four beg something for "us," not for myself alone, but for the whole of humanity. If I pray for all, all pray for me; in fact, the more I forget myself in prayer, the more will God remember me. It is in this spirit that the Lord's Prayer should be recited, meditated on, and lived; one can therefore speak of a "spirituality of the Our Father."

The prayer is transmitted in three sources: Matthew 6:9-13, Luke 11:2-4, and Didache VIII:2. Apart from some minor changes, Luke omits the third and seventh petitions and places the setting of the prayer as a response to the disciples' petition to teach them how to pray as John had instructed his disciples. Moreover, some manuscripts and the Didache add: "For thine is the kingdom, and the power, and the glory, forever. Amen," which corresponds better to the Jewish usage of ending a prayer with praise and blessing. The Lukan version seems to be the oldest. Matthew's community would have inserted the third petition from Jesus' prayer in Gethsemane and the seventh from some tradition which underlies John 17:15.

Calling God "Father" is not new. We find the epithet in Jewish blessings, and the Stoics called Zeus "father" (in the sense in which we speak of "mother earth"). In the Christian context, however, the Father is "The Father of our Lord Jesus Christ," which even in Matthew takes on a Trinitarian connotation (cf. 28:19). God's Fatherhood seems evident, but in times of tribulation, suffering, and death it is not easy to call him Father. Yet it was precisely when dying on the cross that Jesus invoked God as Father (Luke 23:46) and commended his spirit into God's hands.

"Hallowed be thy name" is a passive: by whom? If God's name is already holy who can presume to render it holier? It is true that this phrase can simply mean "may your name be praised by all," a wish. But can it be a petition? In point of fact this is what is called in theological Hebrew a "divine passive," when the passive voice is used to avoid pronouncing the name of God. The subject of the hallowing, therefore, becomes God himself. In the active voice this would be "hallow thy name"; but does this make any sense? We have to turn to the Old Testament to understand its meaning. In Ezekiel 36:16-32 the Lord God blames the exiled Judeans for having profaned his name by means of their idolatry when they were still in their own land. He punished them by letting them go into exile, but even there, instead of rendering witness to their God, they were a scandal to the inhabitants. God therefore decides to act, not for their sake but for the sake of his holy name that they profaned. He himself will sanctify his great name by displaying his holiness among the nations, so that they may know that he is the Lord:

> I will take you from the nations, and gather you from all the countries, and bring you into your own land. I will sprinkle clean water upon you, and you shall be clean from all your uncleannesses, and from all your idols I will cleanse you. A new heart I will give you, and a new spirit I will put within you; and I will remove from your body the heart of stone and give you a heart of flesh. I will put my spirit within you, and make you follow my statutes and be careful to observe my ordinances. Then you shall live in the land that I gave to your ancestors; and you shall be my people, and I will be your God. (36:24-28)

This corresponds to the "new covenant" foretold in Jeremiah 31:31, 33-34:

> The days are surely coming, says the LORD, when I will make a new covenant with the house of Israel and the house of Judah. . . . I will put my law within them, and I will write it on their hearts; and I will be their God, and they shall be my people. No longer shall they teach one another, or say to each other, Know the LORD, for they shall all know me, from the least of them to the greatest, says the LORD; for I will forgive their iniquity, and remember their sin no more.

These prophecies were partly fulfilled on the return from exile, but the full extent of the new covenant had to be inaugurated by Christ's blood (Luke 22:20; 2 Cor. 3:6; Heb. 7:22). When we say, "Hallowed be thy name," therefore, we essentially pray that the Father may gather us from all nations, forgive us our iniquities, cleanse our spirit with clean water, give us his Holy Spirit to turn our hearts of stone into heats of flesh, help us to fulfill his commandments, and make the new covenant effective in Christ. Further, it is interesting to note that the second-century Fathers called Christ "the name" (cf. Phil. 2:9-10), whom God glorified by raising him from the dead, which recalls Jesus' prayer in John 12:28: "'Father, glorify your name.' Then a voice came from heaven, 'I have glorified it, and I will glorify it again,'" and John 17:1: "Father, the hour has come; glorify your Son so that the Son may glorify you." The context of the first invocation of the Lord's Prayer is therefore Christological and ecclesiological: God hallows his name by rendering effective Christ's redemption, and believers respond by living our their vocation in the Holy Spirit within them and by rendering witness to God's Fatherhood in Christ.

The meaning of the second petition, "Thy kingdom come," depends on the various meanings of the kingdom, already discussed earlier in this chapter. It can mean God's offer of forgiveness and reconciliation, his victory over evil, the preaching of the gospel, aspects of the church, the final consummation, or the acknowledgment of God's sovereignty by the whole of humanity. As said above, the kingdom is both present and future, both social and individual. The second invocation can therefore be a subject of meditation in each of these aspects. However, it is always the eschatological aspect that prevails; eschatology does not refer only to the end of world history, it embraces the struggle between good and evil in history leading up to God's final victory, and, in the Christian view, Christ's victory, for God's reign is the risen Christ's sovereignty. This comes to the fore in 1 Corinthians 15 where Paul speaks of Christ's and our resurrection:

> But in fact Christ has been raised from the dead, the first fruits of those who have died. . . . Christ the first fruits, then at his

coming those who belong to Christ. Then comes the end, when he hands over the kingdom to God the Father, after he has destroyed every ruler and every authority and power. For he must reign until he has put all his enemies under his feet. The last enemy to be destroyed is death. For "God has put all things in subjection under his feet" [Ps. 110:1]. . . . When all things are subjected to him, then the Son himself will also be subjected to the one who put all things in subjection under him, so that God may be all in all. (15:20, 23-25, 28)

This apocalyptic theme is taken up in the book of Revelation and repeated with sundry variations especially in its hymns. The coming of God's kingdom is a gift; we do not construct the kingdom, we only respond to its presence among us by collaborating to realize God's plan of salvation. "Thy kingdom come" is the prayer that confesses the hope of all believers. It also expresses the wish that God may reign in every heart, that his church may extend to all peoples, and that the whole cosmos may acknowledge his sovereignty.

"Thy will be done, on earth as it is in heaven." This too can have various meanings. It can be an expression of humble subjection to God's will, as pronounced by Jesus in the garden of olives (Luke 22:42). It can be a prayer for all to follow God's will as expressed in the commandments, or it can have the eschatological meaning of the realization of the history of salvation. The opening chapter of Ephesians is a hymn of thanksgiving to the Father for having chosen believers to the faith: "He has made known to us the mystery of his will, according to his good pleasure that he set forth in Christ, as a plan for the fullness of time, to gather up all things in him, things in heaven and things on earth" (1:9-10). The recapitulation of the whole universe in Christ, the mainstay of the theology of St. Irenaeus, is the goal of God's saving plan for which we pray in this third petition.

We now come to the latter part of the Lord's Prayer and ask: "Give us this day our daily bread." It should be clear that bread stands for all the necessities of life. Luke's Gospel has "Give us each day our daily bread" (11:3), like the manna in the desert. The word "daily" presents some difficulties: the meaning of the Greek *epiousios* is uncertain, for this is the only time it is used in Greek. The early translations of the Gospels render it by means of different expressions, like daily, supernatural, eternal, necessary, future, or tomorrow's. This means that the translators, like the Fathers of the church, did not limit the petition to material bread, for, as the manna had already been interpreted in Deuteronomy, "One does not live by bread alone, but by every word that comes from the mouth of the LORD" (Deut. 8:3). Many Fathers extend the meaning of bread to the Eucharist, which should become the daily nourishment of every Christian. Thus the petition comprehends the whole of the human person, not merely bodily or material necessities. Food, clothing, work, and habitation are important, but how does the Father give us all this? We can certainly speak of providence, but providence comes through human channels. When Jesus observed that the multitude that was listening to the word was hungry, he told his apostles, "You give them something to eat" (Mark 6:37). We can understand this saying much better in our own times when the problem of poverty and undernourishment in the poorer countries comes constantly to the fore. There is enough food for everyone in the world, and when it is lacking God makes use of our scientific discoveries to multiply it. The problem lies not with quantities but with distribution, social justice, and charity. The fourth petition of the Lord's Prayer is therefore a challenge to individuals, social classes, and nations who have an abundance of bread to share it with the more needy. Jesus underlines faith in providence and the danger of over-anxiety in the beautiful passage about the birds of the air and the lilies of the field in Matthew 6:25-34. However, "life" in all its plenitude, is attained by means of material goods, faith in God's word and the Eucharist, and, paradoxically enough, in many cases it is the poor who nourish the rich with their prayers and sufferings.

There is little need to explain what the prayer for forgiveness of debts means. Repentance is a must to enter into the kingdom and no one can say that he has nothing for which to ask forgiveness. We have seen that even the Pharisees, who fast, pray, and observe the precepts, need to beg forgiveness for the intentions that motivate these "good works." "As we also have forgiven our debtors" is a required condition which Jesus repeats at the end: "For if you forgive others their trespasses, your heavenly Father will also forgive you; but if you do not forgive others, neither will your Father forgive your trespasses" (Matt. 6:14-15). It is not God who imitates humans but the latter who follow God's example. Jesus further illustrates this saying by means of the parable of the steward whose debt of ten thousand talents was forgiven because he begged for mercy but who would not release from his debt his fellow steward who owed him only a hundred denarii. As we said above, the coming of the kingdom is a kind of amnesty for the whole of humanity. Since we have been forgiven *a priori* and given the chance of conversion by God, it follows that we should act in a like manner with our neighbor whose debt to us is far below ours to God. Moreover, the past tense used by Matthew means that forgiveness should precede prayer, as Jesus' injunction illustrates: "So when you are offering your gift at the altar, if you remember that your brother or sister has something against you, leave your gift there before the altar and go; first be reconciled to your brother or sister, and then come and offer your gift" (Matt. 5:23-24). Here it is not the other who has harmed us but we who have offended him. If this applies to Jewish sacrifices, how much more does it apply to Christians who receive the Eucharist.

The expression "Lead us not into temptation" often creates misunderstanding. In the New Testament, "temptation" sometimes denotes persecution of Christians or the danger of denying Christ, as in Matthew 26:41; 1 Corinthians 10:13; Revelation 2:2-3, 10. Christians are also tempted as human beings. James warns: "No one, when tempted, should say, 'I am being tempted by God'; for God cannot be tempted with evil and he himself tempts no one. But one is tempted by one's own desire, being lured and enticed by it; then, when that desire has conceived, it gives birth to sin, and that sin, when it is fully grown, gives birth to death" (1:13-15). On the other hand, as *peirazein* can mean "prove, test," God can let us be tempted so that we become aware of our limits, as in the case of Job. Temptations can come from Satan as well (1 Cor. 7:5b; 2 Cor. 2:11; 11:14; 12:7). However, whether we are tempted as Christians or as mere human beings, Paul explains: "No testing has overtaken you that is not common to everyone. God is faithful, and he will not let you be tested beyond your strength, but with the testing he will also provide the way out so that you may be able to endure it" (1 Cor. 10:13). By broadening our views when we recite this invocation we embrace all believers who suffer persecution for their faith or whose faith is tottering, as well as persons who suffer ordinary temptations, from marriages or vocations in crisis to drugs and violence.

As to deliverance from evil, much depends on how we translate the Greek *apo tou ponerou,* a genitive that can be either masculine or neuter, that is, "from the evil one" or "from evil" in general. We may find ourselves already entrapped in evil and therefore beg for deliverance from a particular situation, or feel threatened by evil and ask to be delivered. In John 17:15 Jesus prays that his disciples be delivered or protected from the evil one. At least that is how the phrase is commonly translated, so it is probable that even in the Our Father it bears the same meaning. This invocation presupposes an apocalyptic view of history as the struggle between good and evil, God and chaos, and between Christ and Satan. We pray that we may share in God's final victory already in our own lives.

In this "canonical reading" of the Our Father we have broadened our context to embrace the whole of the New Testament without adhering too strictly to the frame of reference of the historical Jesus. On the other hand the understanding of this prayer grows indefinitely with the ages. This prayer is certainly basic, but we must not forget that the essential act of worship in the church is the Eucharist, to which we now turn our attention.

The Eucharist

For an adequate explanation of the Eucharist we would have to examine, beside the Synoptic account, 1 Corinthians 10 and 11 as well as John 6. In this chapter we shall limit ourselves to the Last Supper as related in the first three Gospels insofar as it relates to spirituality; that is, we shall set aside historical and critical questions that are of little consequence to the understanding of the meaning of the Eucharist for our daily lives.

There are four accounts of the institution of the Last Supper: Matthew 26:26-29; Mark 14:22-25; Luke 22:14-20; and 1 Corinthians 11:23-26. The first two are held to reflect the liturgical usage in Jerusalem; Luke and Paul, the Antiochian celebration. The Gospels agree that the institution took place during the Jewish paschal meal. It is Luke who, by mentioning two cups, best preserves the sequence of the Jewish ceremony.

Let us begin with the words over the bread and the wine. In the Markan and Matthean accounts, before eating the lamb, Jesus takes the bread, pronounces a blessing over it, breaks the loaf and gives it to the apostles saying: "Take, eat, this is my body." Luke and Paul add: "which is given for you. Do this in remembrance of me." Whereas before Jesus, the one presiding over the meal explained every item of food symbolically with reference to the exodus by the Jews, Jesus now gives an original explanation of the bread. In other words he says: Tomorrow I shall be put to death. My death is not accidental; it is a sacrifice I offer to the Father. As you, when you offer your sacrifices, partake of the sacrificed animal to be able to participate in the blessing emanating from the rite, if you want to participate in the atonement my sacrifice effects, you have to eat of my sacrificial flesh.

This you do by eating this bread, which is really my body. In future, you shall repeat this act among yourselves in remembrance of me. What does this remembrance mean? It is not a mere commemoration of the unknown warrior at the cenotaph; remembrance is God's remembrance as Exodus 20:24 explains: "You need make for me only an altar of earth and sacrifice on it your burnt offerings and your offerings of well-being, your sheep, and your oxen; in every place where I cause my name to be remembered I will come to you and bless you." Similarly, if Christ causes his name to be remembered he becomes present and accords his redemptive blessing.

After having eaten the lamb, Jesus blesses the third cup of wine in the ritual and says: "Drink from it, all of you; for this is my blood of the covenant, which is poured out for many for the forgiveness of sins" (Matt. 26:27-28). Luke has: "This cup that is poured out for you is the new covenant in my blood" (22:20). In Exodus 24:8 we read of the way the first covenant was inaugurated: Moses took the blood of sacrificed oxen "and dashed it on the people and said, 'See the blood of the covenant that the LORD has made with you in accordance with all these words.'" Jesus adds "my blood of the new covenant." It is not with animals' blood that the new covenant foretold by Jeremiah and Ezekiel is stipulated, but with Christ's own sacrificial blood. We have already quoted Jeremiah 31:31-34 and Ezekiel 36:24-28. This implies that every time the Eucharist is celebrated the new covenant is renewed. It does not mean that Christ dies again, for "He abolishes the first in order to establish the second. And it is by God's will that we have been sanctified through the offering of the body of Jesus Christ once for all" (Heb. 10:9b-10). It only effects "remembrance" on God's part, as explained above. The second or new covenant raises to a higher, Christological, and ecclesiological level the promises of Jeremiah and Ezekiel every time the Eucharist is celebrated and received. God gathers the church from all nations; he purifies from sin those who believe; he puts his law into their hearts, not as external commandment but as prompted by the Holy Spirit who will also turn their hearts from hearts of stone to hearts of flesh so that they may be able to overcome their weaknesses and be faithful to God's will. Moreover, an explanatory word that follows (in Mark and Matthew) or precedes (in Luke) the words over the bread and wine opens the Supper to an eschatological horizon: "Truly I tell you, I will never again drink of the fruit of the vine until that day when I drink it new in the kingdom of God" (Mark 14:25). Jesus is aware of his imminent death; the prophets had depicted the future kingdom as a succulent meal (cf. Isa. 25:6-9). For Jesus this eschatological meal will take place when the final consummation of the kingdom takes place. Then he will again sit at table with his disciples for a never-ending feast. In the meantime, as an interim anticipation of that day, the disciples sit together with their Lord at the Eucharistic table. "For as often as you eat this bread and drink the cup, you proclaim the Lord's death until he comes" (1 Cor. 11:26).

The Community of Believers

The concepts of kingdom and church do not coincide; rather, the latter is an aspect of the former. The kingdom is not made up of scattered individuals; rather, Jesus intended to give it a certain configuration when he chose the twelve, representing the twelve tribes of Israel, and gave Peter the keys of the kingdom. The disciples were united by a common confession of Jesus as the Christ, the Son of God, and commissioned to preach Jesus' message to the whole world, bearing the consequences he himself had to bear. This community was not a substitute for Israel, but represented the ideal to which Israel was destined to rise in line with the vision of the prophets. The death and resurrection of Christ, subsequent controversies with the Jews, and the entry of the Gentiles together gave the church its definite historical configuration. It is the primary recipient of all that the kingdom stands for. This premise was necessary because New Testament spirituality is not merely a personal commitment, but has an essential community perspective, which we shall portray in the chapters on Paul and John. Here we shall limit ourselves to what Jesus requires of his community as such.

The kingdom "is like a mustard seed that someone took and sowed in the garden; and it grew and became a tree, and the birds of the air made nests in its branches" (Luke 13:19). The Lukan version of this parable (see Mark 4:30-32; Matt. 13:31-32) presupposes the spread of the gospel especially among the Gentiles, and the growth of the church, in spite of all external and internal opposition. Throughout the ages this will be a feature of the church, in which the power of the initial seed is still operative, an encouragement to the "little flock" (Luke 12:32) whose duty it is to spread the kingdom. Other plants, not planted by the Father, are doomed to disappear (Matt. 15:13). The disciples are gathered together above all around a person: "Where two or three are gathered in my name, I am there among them" (Matt. 18:20), a saying that will be repeated after the resurrection when the risen Christ promises to be with his believers to the end of the age (Matt. 28:20). The rabbis taught that wherever two or three were gathered to study the Torah God was present among them. To be gathered in Jesus' name, however, implies acknowledging him as the Christ the Son of God. All four Gospels have Peter's confession as their center (Matt. 16:13-19; Mark 8:29; Luke 9:18-21; John 6:67-71).

Confession and belief without works can be sterile, for "Not every one who says to me, 'Lord, Lord,' will enter the kingdom of heaven, but only the one who does the will of my Father in heaven" (Matt. 7:21). In fact, the guest admitted to the wedding feast of the king's son who was not wearing the wedding garment is scolded and expelled (Matt. 22:11-14). It is in Matthew, who more than the other evangelists reflects on the ecclesial aspect of the kingdom, that Jesus foresees the mixture of good and bad members, as illustrated in the parable of the weeds sown by the devil among the grain (13:24-30) and in the parable of the good and bad fish inside the net (13:47-50).

Such foresight will be of help to all Christians who are upset by scandals occurring within the church. "Woe to the world because of stumbling blocks! Occasions for stumbling are bound to come, but woe to the one by whom the stumbling block comes!" (Matt. 18:7).

The seriousness of the decision to become Jesus' disciple in response to his call is underlined in some sayings of the Master: "Whoever is not with me is against me, and whoever does not gather with me scatters" (Luke 11:23). There cannot be any neutral stance of a mere onlooker in front of the kingdom; one is either for or against. Once the decision is taken there is no looking back, for "No one who puts a hand to the plow and looks back is fit for the kingdom of God" (Luke 9:62). On the other hand, decisions must not be taken in haste, as the series of sayings in Luke 14:28-35 warns: one cannot begin to build a tower without calculating the costs of the whole construction and be compelled to stop in the middle, thus becoming an object of ridicule. Nor can a king go into battle with forces half of those of his opponent. However, as Jesus' call contains in itself the power of the kingdom, it will also help to overcome the difficulties of the decision and all it entails: "From everyone to whom much has been given, much will be required" (Luke 12:48).

What will be required in the first place is that disciples not retain the gifts of the kingdom for themselves alone but share them with those who have not yet heard or accepted the gospel. We call this "mission," which is an integral part in the spreading of God's kingdom. Jesus sent the twelve, two by two, to preach repentance already during his lifetime, giving them power over unclean spirits (Mark 6:7-13), but he was aware that not all would hearken to their appeal. This served as a training for their final sending by the risen Christ in Matthew 28:18-20. Luke (10:1-12) broadens the number of disciples sent to proclaim the gospel to seventy-two. It is not only the "apostles" nor their successors who are charged with the mission to the whole world but the whole church, lay people included, represented by the seventy-two disciples. All in turn represent Christ, for whoever hears them hears Christ (Luke 10:16). Jesus is aware that whether it be among Jews or among Gentiles his representatives will have a hard time, for they will be like sheep among wolves (Matt. 10:16), hence the warning to be wise as serpents and innocent as doves (Matt. 10:16). On the other hand, they should not cast the pearls of the kingdom among swine (Matt. 7:6), that is, people who wallow in vice and are so deaf to spiritual values that any presentation of the gospel will be for them only a subject of derision and antagonism. Moreover, they must give gratis what they received gratis (Matt. 10:8), although the worker is worthy of his wages (Luke 10:7), which he will receive from God, as well as from the sustenance of the community.

Following Jesus means following him not only by accepting his message but also by accompanying him on the path of suffering. He came to announce the truth, the truth about ourselves who play hide and seek with truth. We seek it but are afraid to find it, because it may upset our lives, so when Jesus or his disciples present us with its stark reality it frequently provokes revolt, which results in persecution:

> As for yourselves, beware; for they will hand you over to councils; and you will be beaten in synagogues; and you will stand before governors and kings because of me, as a testimony to them. And the good news must first be proclaimed to all the nations. When they bring you to trial and hand you over, do not worry beforehand about what you are to say; but say whatever is given you at that time, for it is not you who speak, but the Holy Spirit. Brother will betray brother to death, and a father his child, and children will rise against parents and have them put to death; and you will be hated by all because of my name. But the one who endures to the end will be saved. (Mark 13:9-13)

For the evangelist, these words were part prophecy, part contemporary events, and so have they been in the whole history of the church. Lack of harassment may be a sign that Christians are becoming too accommodating and not fulfilling their mission as they should. The "false prophets" about whom Jesus speaks in Matthew 7:15 are not only those who subvert the community with false doctrines but also those who try to avert the church from taking a firm stand on certain essential matters. In these circumstances faintheartedness is lethal: "For those who want to save their life will lose it, and those who lose their life for my sake, and for the sake of the gospel, will save it" (Mark 8:35). The mention of salvation in these two texts leads us to the subject of the eschatological viewpoint of Jesus and the Gospels.

Eschatological Spirituality

Eschatological spirituality is found mainly in Jesus' eschatological discourse reported in Mark 13 and its parallels in the other two Synoptics. For the purposes of biblical spirituality we shall put aside, as we have done elsewhere, the critical questions of the formation of this discourse, that is, what goes back to Jesus himself and what is due to the early church or to the evangelists' redaction. We shall consider the text itself as it stands.

Eschatology has changed in meaning these last decades. Preconciliar textbooks of theology often limited it to "the four last things": death, judgment, punishment, and reward, whereas today we understand it to mean also the end, purpose, finality, and meaning of history. Christ is the goal; he is waiting at the other end. Whether this world ends with a bang or with a whimper, as T. S. Eliot puts it, the whole of creation stretches toward Christ. On the individual level, the demise of each one of us certainly comes into the whole scenario, for otherwise the enduring faith and the sufferings of those who belong to the kingdom would make no sense, but these are viewed within the whole universal context of salvation. We shall have more to say about this when we turn to the book of Revelation.

Mark 13 belongs to the genre of rabbinic homilies called *yelammedenu rabbenu*, that is, a homily or a lesson by a rabbi in response to a question posed by his disciples. In fact, when one of Jesus' followers pointed to the grandeur of the temple, Jesus, like Jeremiah (7:1-4, 11-15), predicted its destruction: "Not one stone will be left here upon another; all will be thrown down" (Mark. 13:2), in response to which Peter, James, John, and Andrew ask: "Tell us, when will this be, and what will be the sign that all these things are about to be accomplished?" (v. 4). Jesus sits down, a sign of teaching authority, and delivers his discourse in private to these four. There are endless discussions among scholars about the sources of Mark 13, as Jewish apocalyptic thought was widespread in the first century, and Jewish Christians did not escape its influence. The core of the discourse, however, goes back to Jesus, as is evident from the accusations against him before the high priests (Mark 14:58; see John 2:13-22). Whatever the case, Mark certainly read this discourse in light of contemporary events in the history of Judea around the year 70: the siege of Jerusalem, the flight of the Christians to Pella beyond the Jordan, and the destruction of the city. Was this the end of the world? His contemporaries, both Jews and Jewish Christians, might have thought so, but the main point of the whole chapter is the theme of vigilance. "Watch!" is the key word.

Eschatology, however, is not only about the end of the world, for God's judgment projects itself throughout history, and certain events are meant to be read as signs of the times — hence the mingling and overlapping of the themes of the fall of Jerusalem and the coming of the Son of Man in Mark 13. *Eschaton* means "last," indeed, but it refers to the last period of salvation history, that is, no other chances after this. On the other hand, the coming Son of Man looms at the end like the Pantocrator in the apse of a Byzantine cathedral. His presence and his coming are not a menace; he comes to gather and save his elect from all the ends of the world. A believer does not fear his coming, but rather expects it and prays for it. Jesus warns, however, that the road is full of perils from false prophets and false messiahs (vv. 5-22), who promise salvation and freedom but lead to destruction. First-century Palestine saw many of them and experienced the downfall of the nation of Israel. They abound in the church's history as well: false doctrines, devious ideologies, and personalities who cause upheavals in various ages. They belong to the "signs of the times" summed up by Jesus in the parable of the fig tree which announces the coming of summer by putting forth its leaves (v. 28). These are all historical reflections of the paradigm of the "desolating sacrilege set up where it ought not to be" (v. 14) announced by Jesus. Therefore the stance of the Christian should be like the household of a master who departed on a long journey and whose return is uncertain (vv. 34-36). Though Mark's generation expected an impending return of Christ, the evangelist underlines Jesus' saying, reminding them that that day or that hour "no one knows, neither the angels in heaven, nor the Son, but only the Father" (v. 32). It was not Christ's mission to reveal dates; these are hidden in the mystery of the Father's designs. Jesus only wants us to remain continually on our guard, as anything may happen any minute that can menace or help us on our way to salvation. Eschatological spirituality is therefore a life of watchfulness for Jesus' presence in our lives and our society; apocalyptic spirituality is interpreting our lives and contemporary events as signs of the continuous struggle between good and evil, certain that the coming of the Son of Man will usher in the final victory of God's goodness and grace.

It is a curious fact that Mark 13 does not mention the resurrection of the dead. We know that Jesus spoke of the resurrection as a definite doctrine, siding against the Sadducees with the Pharisees (Mark 12:18-27). We shall find the association of resurrection and parousia in Paul.

Meditating on Jesus' Miracles

Jesus' miracles were no mere acts of beneficence. They certainly did help those who were cured, but they were limited to a chosen few. John calls these miracles "signs," that is, Jesus' action means something and points to something over and above the mere occurrence. Indeed, the narration of the fact in the earliest communities was not a mere chronicle but a sort of interpretation. When these stories reached their written form in the Gospels, they had passed through a period of interpretative oral transmission and were later stamped by the theological outlook of the evangelists. Vatican II, in *Dei Verbum* 2, states that revelation takes place by means of both words and deeds that reciprocally illustrate one another. A banal example may be children's books with an illustration on one page and its story on the page facing it.

Gospel miracles are usually classified in three categories: healing miracles, exorcisms, and nature miracles, like the multiplication of loaves, walking on the water, and raising a dead man.

We find the key to interpreting the healings in Matthew 11:2-6. John the Baptist sends his disciples to Jesus to ask whether he was the one who was to come, that is, the expected Messiah, or whether they should wait for another. Jesus answers: "Go and tell John what you hear and see: the blind receive their sight, the lame walk, the lepers are cleansed, the deaf hear, the dead are raised, and the poor have good news brought to them. And blessed is anyone who takes no offense at me." These words refer to the promised salvation in Isaiah 35:5-6: "Then the eyes of the blind shall be opened, and the ears of the deaf unstopped; then the lame shall leap like a deer, and the tongue of the speechless sing for joy." This means that the signs of messianic times are there for all to see. The miracles witness to Jesus' messianic mission and to the coming of the kingdom.

The exorcisms, too, point in the same direction. They indicate Christ's victory over Satan and evil: "If it is by the finger of God that

I cast out the demons, then the kingdom of God has come to you. When a strong man, fully armed, guards his castle, his property is safe. But when one stronger than he attacks him and overpowers him, he takes away his armor in which he trusted and divides his plunder" (Luke 11:20-22). The final battle between good and evil has begun, and Christ's victory is assured.

As to the nature miracles, the key to their interpretation lies in Old Testament symbolism. Storms, for example, usually mean chaos in history, the multiplication of loaves refers to the manna in the desert, etc.

It is John, however, who best elaborates the symbolism of Jesus' miracles. We shall have more to say about this in the chapter on John's spirituality. Unlike Mark, he only relates a few wonders: the wedding at Cana (2:1-12), the prophecy to the Samaritan woman (4:7-42), the healing of the official's son (4:46-54), the paralytic at the pool (5:1-9), the multiplication of loaves (6:1-15), Jesus walking on the waters (6:16-21), the healing of the man born blind (9:1-41), the resurrection of Lazarus (11:1-45), and the miraculous draft of fishes (21:1-13). The way John structures the narration of some of these miracles reveals his understanding of the event. The wonder is followed by an "I am" saying of Jesus and a confession of faith. The multiplication of loaves is followed by the saying "I am the bread of life"; to the Samaritan woman Jesus reveals himself, "I am he"; after the healing of the man born blind Jesus says that he is the light of the world; he reveals himself as the resurrection and the life after raising Lazarus. The highest confession of faith, of course, is Thomas's "My Lord and my God." As John's Gospel relates the events of Jesus on earth with an eye on his presence as the risen Christ, this Gospel teaches us that the wonders Jesus worked in Palestine two thousand years ago are "signs" of what the risen Christ is still doing in heaven on a spiritual level. Whoever can read these signs will also end up with a confession of Jesus as the Christ, the Son of God, or other messianic attributes.

If the purpose of "signs" is to reveal the person and the activity of the risen Christ, believers today will keep an eye on the wonders of the spiritual world surrounding them and read them in light of Jesus' signs on earth.

Passion and Death

Millions of Catholics have found solace in the devotion called "The Way of the Cross." The pope himself prays the Stations of the Cross in public on Good Friday. This devotion involves meditating on the details of the passion, from the condemnation to the death and entombment of Jesus, by placing oneself in his stead as he was judged, scorned, scourged, crowned with thorns, nailed, and hung on the cross. Sharing his experience in this way has been valued by numerous mystics, and the experience is especially meaningful if one keeps in mind that it is not merely Jesus as an individual who is suffering but the whole of humankind that he aggregates to himself. The evangelists not only relate the details of the passion, but also enrich them with biblical references and quotations to bring out their significance.

Yet though not unaware of the details of the passion, Paul goes deeper into the meaning of Christ's humiliation and death as an example for all believers. We shall speak of his Christ-mysticism in the next chapter. Here suffice it to recall a couple of passages that reveal the place of the passion in the apostle's teaching. He considered his own sufferings for the gospel as "sharing [Christ's] sufferings by becoming like him in his death" (Phil. 3:10). As we all form one single body in Christ, "if one member suffers, all suffer together with it" (1 Cor. 12:26), much more do we share the sufferings of the head of this body. Indeed, "in my flesh I am completing what is lacking in Christ's afflictions for the sake of his body, that is, the church" (Col. 1:24). He says of his bruises: "I carry the marks of Jesus branded on my body" (Gal. 6:17). Moreover, Paul exhorts the Philippians to "let the same mind be in you that was in Christ Jesus." He summarizes this "mind" in the well-known hymn in Philippians 2:5-11. In this passage he opposes Christ's humility to Adam's pride. Whereas the latter, being a mere human, refused subjection and aspired to become like God, and all he gained was death and return to dust, Christ, who was by nature God, humbled himself not only by becoming human but also by accepting obedience unto death, the death of a crucified slave. For this he was exalted and given the name of God himself, that of "Lord." This should be "the mind" of every believer who takes seriously Christ's incarnation and death.

Conclusion

Both John the Baptist and Jesus began their ministries with the same message: "Repent, for the kingdom of heaven has come near" (Matt. 3:2), but Jesus adds: "and believe in the good news" (Mark 1:15). The kingdom of God, announced by the prophets "in many and various ways" (Heb. 1:1), and eagerly expected but interpreted in diverse ways by Jesus' and John's contemporaries, is God's initiative to restore his initial purpose of creation, thwarted by the rebellion of human beings. The preliminaries of this kingdom are to be found in the whole history of Israel, to whom God reveals his universal Kingship. Now the time has arrived for God to take matters in hand and establish his sovereignty in an effective manner. It is an unmerited gift, and must be received as such. Repentance means a U-turn of someone who has lost his way in the desert and whose only hope of survival is to turn back on his own footsteps. Of course one must believe in the coming of the kingdom and believe him who announces it. As far as we know, John worked no miracles, yet he spoke with the authority of the old prophets whose sole word sufficed to convince those who would hear. Jesus' gospel was much more than a call for repentance; from it emanated the power and the signs of salvation that were the foretaste of the kingdom in all its plenitude. Hence belief in the gospel called for faith in Jesus himself. In the context of the Synoptics, faith often means trust, especially in the context of the miracle stories, but the awe aroused by the miracle in many cases led to the confession of Jesus as the Messiah or the Son of God. Faith, therefore, is that required for one to partake of the gifts of the kingdom as well as the grateful response to their reception. John the Baptist announced the coming of the kingdom. Jesus, insofar as he was the Father's gift to the world, was the kingdom in person, because he was the epitome of God's plan of salvation.

Miracles were the Father's witness to the authenticity of Jesus' gospel; but the final seal on both the word and the person of Jesus was the resurrection. The meaning of the resurrection will be deepened in the preaching of the apostles; in the Gospels it is the vindication of Jesus' rejection and condemnation. Meditating Christ's passion and death is indeed necessary, but the pivot of the Christian faith is the resurrection, for "if Christ has not been raised, then our proclamation has been in vain and your faith has been in vain" (1 Cor. 15:14).

4

Response to the Paschal Mystery: The Pauline Tradition

For the purpose of this study we shall take into account not only Romans, 1 and 2 Corinthians, Galatians, Philippians, Philemon, and 1 Thessalonians, whose authenticity is beyond doubt, but also Ephesians, Colossians, and 2 Thessalonians, which certainly represent genuine Pauline tradition, as well as the Pastoral Letters, as they too reflect the apostle's principles. We shall include some references to Hebrews simply because it belongs traditionally to the Pauline corpus, though it is obviously a letter on its own.

These letters were occasional; they were written for specific purposes, and therefore they do not provide a complete picture either of Paul's theology or of his spirituality, but they do permit us to penetrate to a certain depth into the workings of the writer's mind and to discern the spirit that prompted the letters' composition.

Paul was a Jew, a rabbi belonging to the sect of the Pharisees, who was born and bred in Asia Minor. He was therefore conversant with the Bible, with rabbinic reasoning, and also with such Hellenistic thought as he could glean from the orators who frequented the streets and forums of most cities, propagating the teachings of the various philosophical schools. He must have often observed that many of the ideas in circulation, especially those of the Stoics, were not only not opposed to but even compatible with his own moral principles as a Christian. No wonder then that an apocryphal writing has reached us envisaging an exchange of letters between Paul and Seneca. We shall encounter traces of these thoughts in the rational motivations on which the apostle bases some of his ethical exhortations.

A mention of Paul's name brings to mind his teaching on justification by faith. Indeed, in two of his most important letters, Romans and Galatians, this is the main theme, but that was due to the circumstances that led to the writing of those two epistles. Rightist Jewish Christians, not to speak of Jews, found it hard to accept Paul's main thesis that the law of Moses, which they had practiced with so must sacrifice and scruple, was insufficient for justification, that is, for placing us in right relationship with God; faith in Christ would do that, even in the case of Gentiles who were called to the faith. The controversies arising at the time of the Reformation enhanced this conviction. However, the very fact that it is faith in Christ that justifies is a witness to the fact that central to Paul's thought was Christ, his sacrifice on the cross, and his resurrection from the dead, and that to Paul justification is a corollary.

In fact, we find the essence of the apostle's kerygma, the ice-breaking discourse presenting Christianity to outsiders, in two passages: [Others] "report . . . how you turned to God from idols, to serve a living and true God, and to wait for his Son from heaven, whom he raised from the dead — Jesus, who rescues us from the wrath that is coming" (1 Thess. 1:9-10). "Now I would remind you, brothers and sisters, of the good news that I proclaimed to you. . . . For I handed on to you as of first importance what I in turn had received: that Christ died for our sins in accordance with the scriptures, and that he was buried, and that he was raised on the third day in accordance with the scriptures" (1 Cor. 15:1-4). This is what is called the "indicative" of apostolic preaching; the "imperative," the moral response, is so intertwined with doctrine as to render it inextricable. Even though moral exhortation, as in Romans 12–16, may occupy the concluding part of the letter, it does not stand on its own, as it refers continually to preceding doctrinal themes.

Paul's moral teaching is not a list of Christian precepts to substitute for Old Testament directives. There is a bottom line, of course, below which only absolute condemnation is to be found: "Do not be deceived! Fornicators, idolaters, adulterers, male prostitutes, sodomites, thieves, the greedy, drunkards, revilers, robbers — none of these will inherit the kingdom of God" (1 Cor. 6:9b-10). Paul's exhortations exhibit positive values, consisting of virtues and dispositions centered on love, the response of love to the love of God which overflows to love of neighbor: "For the whole law is summed up in a single commandment, 'You shall love your neighbor as yourself.' . . . Bear one another's burdens, and in this way you will fulfill the law of Christ" (Gal. 5:14; 6:2).

We can now turn to the values and virtues to be found in the parenetic passages of these letters. For the purpose of this chapter on Pauline spirituality, rather than providing lists of recommendations it is more profitable to inquire into the motivations and principles that gave rise to and animated these exhortations, for these will lead us to the root of the author's reasoning and help us to learn to think in the same way. We shall underline in a special manner those motivations rooted in Christology and salvation history, which distinguish Pauline morality from that of the Stoics and from rabbinic rules of behavior.

We shall begin, however, with those axioms common to all, common sense first and foremost, expressed in the form of proverbs, gnomic sayings, and psychological observations. In 2 Thessalonians 3:10 lazy members of the community are warned that "Anyone unwilling to work should not eat." One Corinthians is full of such principles: "A little yeast leavens the whole batch of dough" (5:6) is applied to the scandalous behavior of the man living with his stepmother. A soldier is worthy of his pay, so are those who work in the Lord's vineyard (9:7, 10). It is absurd for a woman to shave off her hair (11:15f.). Fathers should not be too harsh with their children lest they lose heart (Col. 3:21). This way of reasoning is often found in Old Testament wisdom sayings and in the *halakha*.

A sense of shame can also motivate behavior. The Thessalonians should be ashamed to exercise sexuality in a pagan way (1 Thess. 4:4-5); the Corinthians must be generous in their donations for the Jerusalem community so as not to cause Paul to blush when he goes to Macedonia (2 Cor. 9:4); Jews who boast of the law and consider themselves teachers of morality should be ashamed to behave worse than the Gentiles (Rom. 2).

Purely social reasons also concern Christian morality. Christians shall live in peace with everyone so that they may gain the respect of outsiders (1 Thess. 4:12); they shall be subject to the civil powers whose authority derives from God (Rom. 13:1-7); Christians must not disparage others lest they destroy one another (Gal. 5:15); thieves should no longer rob, but work with their own hands to help the needy (Eph. 4:28). Paul is not concerned directly with social questions; like any other Jew he was convinced that by observing God's law, order and peace would be established in the community. Christians were a foreign body living in a pagan world; he believed a change in society would be brought about by the principles and values they preached. Nor were they to cause any revolution; in fact, Paul accepted slavery and the household hierarchy as they stood — indeed, he sent back the runaway slave Onesimus to his master — but by insisting on the equality of all persons before God he believed slavery was bound to fall by itself.

The reward and punishment motive is to be found in the whole Bible. This theme does not refer to eschatological salvation or damnation but to what scholars call "divine right sayings," which means that an action carries within itself its reward or punishment, indicative of God's presence in his commandments. For example, "If anyone destroys God's temple, God will destroy that person. For God's temple is holy, and you are that temple" (1 Cor. 3:17); "All who eat and drink without discerning the body [Eucharist], eat and drink judgment against themselves" (1 Cor. 11:29); "Let anyone be accursed who has no love for the Lord" (1 Cor. 16:22). These are not meant as threats to produce fear; they just assert that there are fixed points in morality that are not to be tampered with.

More positive is the motivation for the performance of good deeds that are pleasing to God: a person should pray, be joyful, and render thanks because these things please God (1 Thess. 5:16-18); the virgin with an undivided heart seeks to please God in every way (1 Cor. 7:32-35); God loves a joyful giver (2 Cor. 9:6-9); children should obey their parents because this is pleasing to God (Col. 3:20).

The Pauline writings are full of citations from or allusions to the Old Testament. In his parenetic passages Paul does not usually deduce rules of moral behavior from the Bible as the rabbis did, either by means of direct exegesis *(peshat)* or through a complex hermeneutical process called *derash*. His morality is Christian, but he very often reinforces his exhortations with references to the Bible to demonstrate that his teachings do not contradict the Old Testament with which the Jewish-Christians and the "God-fearers" — Gentiles who had frequented the synagogues without becoming Jewish — were so familiar.

The motives adduced in the preceding paragraphs could also have belonged to Hellenistic moral teaching or to rabbinic *halakha*. Christian spirituality has its own motivations based on the new status of the baptized Christian and his or her relationship with Christ. Conversion to Christianity is not merely a moral change of behavior; this is both a prerequisite and a consequence. What baptism in Christ does in the neophyte is to effect an ontological change of personality: "Put on the Lord Jesus Christ, and make no provision for the flesh, to gratify its desires" (Rom. 13:14). A Christian, therefore, is not just one who follows the doctrine of Jesus as a Platonist is one who follows Plato; rather, a person "becomes" Christ insofar as he or she is now incorporated into Christ's body. "We know that our old self was crucified with him so that the body of sin might be destroyed, and we might no longer be enslaved to sin. . . . But if we have died with Christ, we believe that we will also live with him" (Rom. 6:6, 8). Our whole *forma mentis* and our behavior will now conform to the nature of the risen Christ. Paul draws further conclusions from this basic premise; for example, he appeals to those who caused divisions in Corinth with the words: "Do you not know that you are God's temple, and that God's Spirit dwells in you? . . . You belong to Christ, and Christ belongs to God" (1 Cor. 3:16, 23). When the apostle prohibits sleeping with a prostitute his reasons are that our body is now a member of Christ, a temple of the Holy Spirit; it will be raised again from the dead, so it no longer belongs to us but to Christ, by whom it was bought dearly (1 Cor. 6:13b-20). In Romans 14:23 Paul discusses the questions of certain foods prohibited to Jews but not to Gentile Christians that were causing scandal and separation. He concludes: "Whatever does not proceed from faith is sin." He does not use here the usual word for conscience, *syneidesis* as in 1 Corinthians 8:10, but *pistis,* faith; for, apart from his human conscience the Christian acquires a new conscience, which is the result of his faith.

The next group of motivations is drawn from the entire history of salvation, from the creation stories in Genesis through the exodus to the sending of God's Son. Paul's insistence in 1 Corinthians 11:5-16 that women should wear a veil is based on Genesis 2. The Corinthians who still offered sacrifices to idols, perhaps because they belonged to some corporation whose meetings were always preceded by a sacrifice, and lack of participation would have had them expelled, are warned by means of the example of the punishments incurred by the Israelites during the exodus because they had succumbed to idol worship (1 Cor. 10:1-10). Yet the most brilliant example of how Paul based even his lesser decisions on salvation history is to be found in 2 Corinthians 1:17-22. He had been accused of not having kept his word to visit the Corinthian community. He replies giving the practical reasons why he had not done so, but then continues:

> Do I make my plans according to ordinary human standards, ready to say "Yes, yes" and "No, no" at the same time? As surely as God is faithful, our word to you has not been "Yes and No." For the Son of God, Jesus Christ, whom we proclaimed among you . . . was not "Yes and No"; but in him it is always "Yes." For in him every one of God's promises is a "Yes." For this reason it is through him that we say the "Amen," to the glory of God. But it is God who establishes us with you in Christ, and has anointed us, by putting his seal on us and giving us his Spirit in our hearts as a first installment.

This is actually a Trinitarian argument, involving the Father, his Son, and the Spirit. The sending of the Son is God's "Yes" to all God's promises and is a model for our promises as well. Perhaps the apostle is recalling the word of Jesus about a Yes being a Yes and a No being a No (Matt. 5:37).

Apart from immediate reward and punishment in the "sentences of divine right" mentioned above, eschatology plays a major role in Paul's exhortations. It is often said that the apostle's expectation of an imminent parousia was the mainspring of his moral teaching. Paul did anticipate the return of the Lord, even in his own lifetime, but had he known that this would not occur for thousands of years his preaching likely would not have altered much. Whether the end of the world is imminent or not, believers must always confront themselves with the end of history and God's final judgment. Going along with the finality and purpose of history in God's mind is the practical consequence of both the Christian's faith and his hope. Hence the Thessalonians are exhorted to put on the armor of Christian virtues, "for God has destined us not for wrath, but for obtaining salvation through our Lord Jesus Christ, who died for us, so that whether we are awake or asleep we may live with him" (1 Thess. 5:9-10). We have already mentioned the resurrection as the destiny of the body as an argument against prostitution in 1 Corinthians 6:9-20. Again in Romans 16:19b-20: "I want you to be wise in what is good and guileless in what is evil. The God of peace will shortly crush Satan under your feet." Order in the Christian household is motivated in Colossians 3:23-25 with the words: "Whatever your task, put yourselves into it, as done for the Lord and not for your masters, since you know that from the Lord you will receive the inheritance as your reward. . . . For the wrongdoer will be paid back for whatever wrong has been done, and there is no partiality."

We have already seen that the Christian belongs to society at large, which imposes certain duties on him, but that first and foremost he belongs to the church, Christ's mystical body. The relationships within this body are quite different from those in civil society, as were relationships within Israel, and more particularly in Qumran, for Jews. Paul often appeals to the ecclesial conscience of believers in his parenesis. Here are some examples. In the Eucharistic celebration of the Corinthian community there were some blatant inequalities; the Lord's Supper took place in the context of an *agape*, a meal in which the mutual love of the members of the community should have expressed itself. What happened instead was that while the members were waiting for others to arrive, the rich began eating whatever they had brought with them instead of sharing with their poorer brethren. Paul upbraids them: "Do you not have homes to eat and drink in? Or do you show contempt for the church of God and humiliate those who have nothing?" (1 Cor. 11:22). Again one of the tasks of Paul's ministry was to make a collection to be sent from the believers in the diaspora to the poorer church of Jerusalem, mother of all the churches. The apostle exhorts to generosity: "I do not mean that there should be relief for others and pressure on you, but it is a question of a fair balance between your present abundance and their need, so that their abundance may be for your need, in order that there may be a fair balance" (2 Cor. 8:13-14). There is therefore an exchange of goods; the material goods of the Corinthians are repaid with the spiritual riches of the mother church. Further, in Ephesians, the writer begs the believers to lead a life worthy of their calling, for he is eager to maintain the unity of the Spirit in the bond of peace:

> There is one body and one Spirit, just as you were called to the one hope of your calling, one Lord, one faith, one baptism, one God and Father of all, who is above all and through all and in all. But each of us was given grace according to the measure of Christ's gift. . . . We must no longer be children, tossed to and fro and blown about by every wind of doctrine, by people's trickery, by their craftiness and deceitful scheming. But speaking the truth in love, we must grow up in every way into him who is the head, into Christ, from whom the whole body, joined and knit together by every ligament with which it is equipped, as each part is working properly, promotes the body's growth in building itself up in love. (Eph. 4:4-7, 14-16)

Further on, treating the subject of household relationships, the author founded the loving union between husband and wife on that between Christ and the church, his spouse (Eph. 5:24).

Till now we have enumerated diverse motives that led Paul and his school to build a suitable ethic for Christians. Some of these motives were common to Greeks, Jews, and Christians, though the last three we examined are typically Christian. We shall now pass on to examine other texts with a distinctively Christological motivation. They range from the personal relationship of the believer with Christ, through Christ's presence in the Christian, to imitation of Christ and God.

In 1 Corinthians 1:13 Paul shows his displeasure for the divisions or parties present in the Corinthian community, groups siding with various apostles. He expostulates: "Has Christ been divided? Was Paul crucified for you? Or were you baptized in the name of Paul?" The neophyte is baptized into Christ, the preacher is only a messenger; as Christ is one, so is his body. It tolerates no division. Further on in chapter 3 the apostle takes up the argument once more. It seems that the rhetorical preaching of Apollos from Alexandria had impressed some of the Corinthians; they thought that they had attained to a higher gnosis, or knowledge, disdaining Paul's blunt evangelization. In vv. 18, 21-22 he writes: "If you think that you are wise in this age, you should become fools so that you may become wise. . . . So let no one boast about human leaders. For all things are yours, whether Paul or Apollos of Cephas or the world or life or death or the present or the future — all belong to you, and you belong to Christ, and Christ belongs to God." Human wisdom is folly before God; faith in a crucified Christ, despised by the "wise of this world," is true wisdom. All are united in this faith, apostles and believers, and all belong to Christ, who, in turn, belongs to God.

We have already mentioned the case of members of the community who went to prostitutes (perhaps "sacred prostitution" around Venus's temple on the Acrocorinth). Paul's reason for reprehending them is: "Do you not know that your bodies are members of Christ? Should I therefore take the members of Christ and make them members of a prostitute? . . . Anyone united to the Lord becomes one spirit with him. . . . Every sin that a person commits is outside the body; but the fornicator sins against the body itself," that is, the body of Christ to which he belongs as he was bought with a price (6:15-20).

Broad-minded Corinthians who had understood Paul's message had no scruples about eating meat that had been offered in sacrifice in a pagan temple and later sold in the market; those who came from Judaism, however, would never touch those foods. The apostle lays down some principles for peaceful community living; he approves of the broader ways of the former with one proviso: if, by your eating, you scandalize your brother in the faith you commit sin, the reason being: "By your knowledge those weak believers for whom Christ died are destroyed. But when you thus sin against members of your family . . . you sin against Christ. Therefore, if food is a cause for their falling, I will never eat meat, so that I may not cause one of them to fall" (1 Cor. 8:11-13).

We spoke in the preceding chapter about the imitation of Christ, and said there that Paul raises that imitation to a theological level. Here are some examples. First of all he exhorts the Corinthians: "Be imitators of me, as I am of Christ." Paul asserts that he did not seek his own advantage, "but that of many, so that they may be saved" (1 Cor. 11:1; 10:33). In 2 Corinthians 8:9 Paul extends imitation to the pre-existent Christ himself when begging the community to be generous with their collection for the poorer brethren: "For you know the generous act of our Lord Jesus Christ, that though he was rich, yet for your sakes he became poor, so that by his poverty you might become rich" (2 Cor. 8:9). This recalls the words to the Philippians about Christ being in the nature of God yet he humbled himself in obedience unto death as a model for the attitudes of believers (Phil. 2:5-8). Through his humiliation Christ obtained power. So does Paul, who may be weak, but possesses Christ's power: "For he was crucified in weakness, but lives by the power of God. For we are weak in him, but in dealing with you we will live with him by the power of God" (2 Cor. 13:4).

It is not only Christ we should imitate, but God himself: "Be kind to one another, tenderhearted, forgiving one another, as God in Christ has forgiven you. Therefore be imitators of God, as beloved children, and live in love, as Christ loved us and gave himself up for us, a fragrant offering and sacrifice to God" (Eph. 4:32–5:2).

The fifth petition of the Our Father is here expanded in the light of the passion and resurrection.

The motif of the imitation of God is to be found among the Stoics, in the Old Testament, and in rabbinic theology. Paul appeals to the saving initiative of the Father in Christ, which constituted the heart of his kerygma.

This list of motivations for correct Christian behavior will help us to identify some values on which Paul insisted most. Being justified by faith instead of by the observance of the Mosaic law was certainly no incentive to lax behavior; indeed, it required a greater involvement to live up to the ideals of positive virtues than to limit oneself to not transgressing a commandment. Striving after these ideals, however, is to let oneself be driven by the dynamism of the Holy Spirit within us, as we shall see later; faith now acts as conscience in the spirit of Jeremiah 31:33-34 who stresses that God will place his law in the hearts of those who belong to the new covenant. It is only full insertion in Christ that fills us with the Spirit, whose temple Christians as individuals and as a body become, the destruction of which would bring destruction on themselves. They "put on" Christ, who effects a transformation from an "Adamic" into a "Christic" personality. This does not mean that so-called believers cannot sink down to the basest of vices, which exclude them from the kingdom of God, that is, from justification in this life and eternal salvation in the next. They corrupt themselves as well as the community. We saw that at the apex of the virtues is love, of God and of neighbor, and that such love summarizes the whole law. Bearing one another's burden knits the community together in Christ, who bore our burden; he redeemed us by dying for us, but full and final redemption is still a thing of the future when he returns to raise us with him and judge the living and the dead. Waiting for the parousia is not an inducement to laziness; each one must earn his own living to be able to maintain himself and help the more needy, the poor who surround us, and the poorer communities. Paul's zeal for the collection to be sent to the mother church of Jerusalem was not motivated by economic needs alone. Rather, to him the collection was a sign of union with the mother church and *koinonia*, a commonwealth of material and spiritual goods circulating within the church as exemplified by the sharing of goods in the Jerusalem community itself (Acts 2 and 4). This mutual help should have created peace within the church, though it sometimes degenerated into rivalry, as we read in Acts. But peace was not only to be valued inside the church; the Christians had to be a sign of peace and peaceful living among both Jews and Gentiles, to the extent of honoring and obeying those very authorities who persecuted them. By this good example they would propagate those values that would one day transform social living. A person's dignity is defined by the phrase "for whom Christ died." Order in society would begin with order within the Christian household; the union between husband and wife, and the behavior of children and slaves, was based on the example of Christ's love for the church and his own obedience unto death. Virginity too provided an ideal of an undivided heart belonging to Christ alone. The Yes of faith and the Yes to others reflect God's Yes to humanity when he sent his Son promised by the prophets, a Yes on which we can rely to lead us to the longed-for goal of "being with Christ." As we already form one body and one spirit with Christ, whoever sins against church unity lacerates Christ and profanes the Eucharist.

The Dynamism of Life in the Spirit

Even with the above synthesis of Christian virtues and values resulting from Paul's motivations we have not yet reached the heart of Paul's spirituality. A list of virtues to be practiced can be "law" in the Pauline sense as would a list of prohibitions. A brief explanation of Romans 7 and 8 will offer us a glimpse of the apostle's anthropology and enable us to understand what dynamic spirituality is.

Some preliminaries: First of all the biblical concepts of "flesh" and "spirit"; these are not identical with "body" and "soul" in our common parlance, as we noted in the introductory chapter. "Flesh" is the whole human person under the aspect of weakness, as opposed to "spirit," which can mean either the life-giving breath within us or a supernatural power given to some in definite circumstances. The Hebrew *ruach,* the Greek *pneuma,* and the Latin *spiritus* can all mean "wind," an invisible power that can sail a ship across the ocean or destroy a house. Second, the word "law" refers primarily to the Torah, the law of Moses, though sometimes it is used in the broader sense of any external precept. Paul never distinguishes between the ceremonial laws and the Ten Commandments, but the list of vices that exclude from the kingdom is based on these commandments. Third, by "sin" Paul does not refer to actual sins, which he usually terms "transgressions"; "sin" is that drive within us that is more powerful than our will and compels us to transgress; the rabbis call it *yetzer ha-ra'* (the evil inclination). For Paul, sin entered the world through Adam's transgression and passed into humankind.

Given these premises, the argument in Romans 7 runs as follows: verses 1-4 argue the Christian's freedom from the law by means of a curious similitude which reveals the author's concept of the body of believers. By law, a woman is bound to her husband while he lives; if he dies, the woman can marry another man. Similarly, we were espoused to our Adamic lineage, but that has died with Jesus' death, so we are now free to espouse another man, the risen Christ, and through that association to bear fruit for God. Therefore the law no longer obliges us. We are no longer slaves of the "flesh," for we possess a new life in the Spirit.

This by no means leads to the conclusion that the law is evil. No, it is "spiritual," supernatural, given by God, but it propounds such a high ideal that humans, whose weakness is dominated by the power of "sin," lose their moral freedom and succumb to transgression. There is a constant struggle inside every human being between what one would like to be and what one actually is. "I see what is good, but I follow what is evil" was already an axiom in the apostle's world. Paul personalizes this conflict, speaking dramatically in the first person: "Wretched man that I am! Who will rescue me from this body of death? Thanks be to God through Jesus Christ our Lord! So then, with my mind I am a slave to the law of God, but with my flesh I am a slave to the law of sin" (7:24-25).

In the chapter that follows, Paul introduces the "law of the Spirit of life in Christ Jesus" (8:2) that restores to us our lost moral freedom. For a better understanding of his argument it is useful to recall two texts to which we referred when speaking of the Eucharist in the previous chapter: Jeremiah 31:31-34 and Ezekiel 36:22-27. Jeremiah promises a new covenant that will consist in placing the law within the human heart. Ezekiel's promise, though not called a new covenant, develops and renders more explicit Jeremiah's text:

> I will take you from the nations, and gather you from all the countries, and bring you into your own land. I will sprinkle clean water upon you, and you shall be clean from all your uncleannesses, and from all your idols I will cleanse you. A new heart I will give you, and a new spirit I will put within you; and I will remove from your body the heart of stone and give you a heart of flesh. I will put my spirit within you, and make you follow my statutes and be careful to observe my ordinances. Then you shall live in the land that I gave your ancestors; and you shall be my people, and I will be your God. (vv. 24-28)

Historically, these words obviously refer to the return from exile, but the "new covenant" theme underwent many subsequent reinterpretations until it reached the New Testament, which received its name from it.

Against this background, Paul develops the topic in Romans 8. "The law of the Spirit of life in Christ Jesus" (8:2) means that the power of the Holy Spirit emanating from the risen Christ floods the believer, endowing him with energy to overcome his weakness as "flesh" to be able to submit willingly to God's behest. Romans 8:3 says that God "condemned sin in the flesh." This is what is called "actual grace," but it is much more, for it is not limited to single actions, but pervades the Christian in such a way that it gradually makes him grow to "the full stature of Christ" (Eph. 4:13). The law of Christ is not an exterior commandment that tells you what to do but leaves you in your weakness. It is meant to become "second nature" within the believer, who chooses that course of action out of God-given wisdom and pure love. It should be evident that this does not happen as soon as the believer is baptized. He does indeed receive the Spirit but he must develop this gift with all his capacity until it reaches full maturity, if it can ever do so perfectly in this life.

It is worthwhile to quote here in full Galatians 5:16-24:

> Live by the Spirit, I say, and do not gratify the desires of the flesh. For what the flesh desires is opposed to the Spirit, and what the Spirit desires is opposed to the flesh; for these are opposed to each other, to prevent you from doing what you want. But if you are led by the Spirit, you are not subject to the law. Now the works of the flesh are obvious: fornication, impurity, licentiousness, idolatry, sorcery, enmities, strife, jealousy, anger, quarrels, dissensions, factions, envy, drunkenness, carousing, and things like these. I am warning you, as I warned you before: those who do such things will not inherit the kingdom of God. By contrast, the fruit of the Spirit is love, joy, peace, patience, kindness, generosity, faithfulness, gentleness, and self-control. There is no law against such things. And those who belong to Christ Jesus have crucified the flesh with its passions and desires.

Paul says of himself: "May I never boast of anything except the cross of our Lord Jesus Christ, by which the world has been crucified to me, and I to the world. . . . From now on, let no one make trouble for me; for I carry the marks of Jesus branded on my body" (Gal. 6:14, 17).

This takes place "in Christ Jesus," a typical Pauline expression defining the status of Christians both individually and as church. The church is "Christ's body" as described in Romans 12:4-5; 1 Corinthians 12:12; Ephesians 1:23 and 4:4; and Colossians 3:15. In Romans 8:9-10 however, we also find the expressions "Christ in us," ourselves "in the Spirit," and "the Spirit within us." How can we combine these phrases to make some sense? We have to force metaphorical language to its greatest extent to help us to form an image in our mind that helps us to understand the logic of these expressions. We borrow this imagery from a body surrounded by a powerful magnetic field. We can picture the risen Christ, standing at the right hand of the Father emitting the Spirit received from him within the range of his "glory." Those who receive this Spirit are penetrated by it, hence they are "in the Spirit" and "the Spirit is in them"; at the same time they are "in Christ" because they are one body with him, and "Christ is in them" through his Spirit. Christ's glory, often represented in the Bible by a luminous cloud all around God, is the dynamic field of his saving power that draws everything to him who was exalted on the cross and in heaven (John 12:32).

The effects of the dwelling of the Spirit in the believer are enumerated in Romans 8:9-17: he belongs to Christ, his spirit is alive in righteousness, he will be raised with Christ, he is not subject to the flesh and becomes a son of God, whom he can now address as "Abba." Verses 18-24, however, speak of the sufferings of the world in which the Christian is immersed, as a creature and as a believer, for the cosmos itself yearns for deliverance, as humankind's sin has subjected it to slavery. Lastly, the Spirit "intercedes for us" in prayer (vv. 26-27) in the sense that it enlightens us to pray to God for the right things according to his saving will, not "according to the flesh," thus overcoming the disorientation of our minds regarding the object of our petition. Paul's letters are interspersed with prayers and requests for prayer on behalf of and from his churches, especially at the beginning and end of the epistle. He wants to create a network of prayer among all his congregations with the aim of furthering church unity, spreading the gospel, being saved from opponents, and advancing in maturity of faith. There is therefore a circular movement of petition uniting believers and the apostle with each other, with God and the risen Christ. All this is made possible through the presence of the Holy Spirit in the community.

Paul's Christ- and Spirit-mysticism does not limit itself to individuals. In fact, the individual person is endowed with the Spirit as one who is "in Christ," that is, as one who belongs to Christ's body, the church. The Spirit is the agent of revelation (1 Cor. 2:10-15), and of the unity of this body, by endowing it with diverse charisms thus giving it an organic structure (Rom. 12 and 1 Cor. 12); he unites all with the bond of love (1 Cor. 13), the soul of all charisms, for "God's love has been poured into our hearts through the Holy Spirit that has been given to us" (Rom. 5:5). This "Love is patient; love is kind; love is not envious or boastful or arrogant or rude. It does not insist on its own way; it is not irritable or resentful; it does not rejoice in wrongdoing, but rejoices in the truth. It bears all things, believes all things, hopes all things, endures all things" (1 Cor. 13:4-7).

I end this section illustrating Paul's personal mysticism by means of a few quotations from the Epistle to the Philippians. In this tranquil letter the apostle opens his heart to his preferred community: "For to me living is Christ and dying is gain" (1:21); "For he has graciously granted you the privilege not only of believing in Christ, but of suffering for him as well — since you are having the same struggle that you saw I had and now hear that I still have" (1:29-30). Paul confesses that he is a blameless observer of the law:

> Yet whatever gains I had, these I have come to regard as loss because of Christ. More than that, I regard everything as loss be-

cause of the surpassing value of knowing Christ Jesus my Lord. For his sake I have suffered the loss of all things, and I regard them as rubbish, in order that I may gain Christ and be found in him, not having a righteousness of my own that comes from the law, but one that comes through faith in Christ, the righteousness from God based on faith. I want to know Christ and the power of his resurrection and the sharing of his sufferings by becoming like him in his death, if somehow I may attain the resurrection from the dead. Not that I have already obtained this or have already reached the goal; but I press on to make it my own, because Christ Jesus has made me his own. Beloved, I do not consider that I have made it my own; but one thing I do: forgetting what lies behind and straining forward to what lies ahead, I press on toward the goal for the prize of the upward call of God in Christ Jesus. Let those of us then who are mature be of the same mind. (3:7-15)

The Epistle to the Hebrews

Though certainly not Paul's, this letter has long been associated with him. It merits due consideration for its spiritual outlook, based on the sacrifice and priesthood of Christ as the foundation of the new covenant. We find various opinions among scholars regarding the author, time, and circumstances of the writing of this letter. In my opinion, the most probable working hypothesis is that the epistle was written immediately after the fall of Jerusalem to a community of Jewish Christians in or around Rome, some of whose members were in crisis because of the recent fall of Jerusalem and of the temple, to which they were still strongly attached. The ground was giving way under their feet, as it was in the case of the Jews. This despondency threatened their faith in Christ and many were in danger of going back to Judaism in solidarity with their Jewish brethren, whom they felt they had deserted. The author intends to convince them that the temple with its cult is now of no importance to Christians as there is one High Priest and one sacrifice, Christ who inhabits the heavenly temple, the New Jerusalem, towards which God's people are marching, subject to all the temptations Israel had in the desert on its way to the Promised Land (cf. 1 Cor. 10:1-10). Such a definite historical circumstance finds its analogy in our times as well, when many Christians, disheartened when they look at the turmoil in societies, religions, and philosophies that surround them, tend to give up and fall into the welcoming arms of an agnostic world. Their doubts are strengthened by erroneous ideas about a static church. The exhortations in Hebrews, therefore, with its teaching on the dynamism of a people on the march, are of actual value to us.

The last chapters in the Pauline epistles are usually parenetic, and so are the last two chapters in Hebrews, but moral exhortations in this letter are also spread throughout its doctrinal parts. What then is the relationship between doctrine and parenesis in this letter?

The letter opens with a very condensed confession of faith, comparable with John's prologue and Romans 1:1-3. This is followed by a number of Old Testament quotations showing Christ's superiority over the angels. One may ask why there is such emphasis on a fact that should have been obvious to the addressees. It may be that there was angel worship among them as among the Colossians, but we obtain a better answer from 2:1-4, a strong *a fortiori* argument: beware of neglecting the salvation of the Lord, for if the revelation to Moses, given by angels, received just retribution, what do they deserve who neglect the Lord's grace, attested by eyewitnesses, witnessed by signs and wonders in the community, and confirmed by the charisms of the Holy Spirit? The exalted Son of Man in Psalm 8, whose brethren we have become because he shared our nature, will subject everything under his feet (cf. 1 Cor. 15:25-28). The long quotation from

Psalm 95 in 3:7-11 illustrates the "just retribution" of unbelieving Jews: they did not enter "God's rest," the promised land. The land into which Joshua led his people was not "God's rest," the protological and eschatological sabbath in Genesis 1; another chance has been given to us, "today," the period between the resurrection and the consummation. Now Christ is superior not only to the angels but also to Moses, who was merely a servant in God's house, while Christ is Son and heir, and we ourselves are God's household.

This long and complicated argument, which unites the exodus motif, Christology, and revelation, leads to the severe warning and exhortation in 4:11-13: "Let us therefore make every effort to enter that rest, so that no one may fall through such disobedience as theirs. Indeed, the word of God is living and active, sharper than any two-edged sword, piercing until it divides soul from spirit, joints from marrow; it is able to judge the thoughts and intentions of the heart. And before him no creature is hidden, but all are naked and laid bare to the eyes of the one to whom we must render an account."

The verses that follow introduce the central theme of the high priesthood of Christ, differing in kind both from the hereditary Aaronic priesthood and from the sacrificial victim, Christ's own self. The author of the letter is aware that the argument is difficult — in fact he wants his hearers to pass on from milk to solid food (5:12, 14) — but it is a necessary argument in the present circumstances of the fall of Jerusalem to convince the Jewish Christians that the destruction of the temple did not affect the faith of Christians, for the true cult has now been transferred to the heavenly Jerusalem. Indeed, 6:4-6 has a dire warning for those who slide back into Judaism after having experienced the gift of the new covenant: "For it is impossible to restore again to repentance those who have once been enlightened, and have tasted the heavenly gift, and have shared in the Holy Spirit, and have tasted the goodness of the word of God and the powers of the age to come, and then have fallen away, since on their own they are crucifying again the Son of God and are holding him up to contempt." This is only a warning, for the author continues saying that it is not the case of his readers, whose good works and steadfastness are known by all: may they persevere in this disposition. We meet the same warning but also the same words of praise and encouragement in 10:19-39, following the long section about the priesthood of Christ, entirely different from the Aaronic priesthood, and his self-immolation as obedience, in the words of Psalm 40:6-8, which opens the era of the new covenant foretold by Jeremiah (3:31-34; see also Ezek. 36:26ff.). The old covenant is becoming obsolete and ready to disappear (8:13), so why go back to it after having found joy and endured suffering in the new faith? This would only merit inexorable judgment.

Chapter 11 is a fine example of the author's hermeneutic of faith, illustrated according to the genre *exempla patrum*, by numerous examples of the faith of the patriarchs. It opens with a definition: "Now faith is the assurance of things hoped for, the conviction of things not seen." One sees immediately that for this author faith is forward-looking, equivalent to hope, but based on the conviction that things unseen are more real than the perceptible world. He adduces the examples of Abel, Enoch, Noah, Abraham, Sarah, Moses, Rahab, the judges, Samuel, and David. His occasional comments reveal his concept of faith as the driving force of a people marching toward a goal that for them is more real than the difficulties they are experiencing. We quote some examples: "By faith Abraham obeyed when he was called to set out for a place that he was to receive as an inheritance; and he set out, not knowing where he was going. . . . For he looked forward to the city that has foundations, whose architect and builder is God" (vv. 8, 10); "All these died in faith without having received the promises, but from a distance they saw and greeted them. They confessed that they were strangers and foreigners on the earth" (v. 13); "By faith Moses, when he was grown up, refused to be called a son of Pharaoh's daughter, choosing rather to share ill-treatment with the people of God than to enjoy the fleeting pleasures of sin. He considered abuse suffered for the Christ to be greater wealth than the treasures of Egypt, for he was looking ahead to the reward" (vv. 24-26); "Yet all these, though they were commended for their faith, did not receive what was promised, since God had provided something better so that they would not, apart from us, be made perfect" (vv. 39-40). The crowning example is that of Jesus, "the pioneer and perfecter of our faith, who for the sake of the joy that was set before him endured the cross, disregarding its shame, and has taken his seat at the right hand of the throne of God" (12:2). Chapter 12:3-13 continues with an exhortation to endurance, to consider the sufferings of his readers as the discipline of a loving father towards a child he wants to bring to maturity.

The forward-looking conviction of faith requires a clear eschatology. In 12:18-24 the author recalls the fear and trembling at the foot of Mount Sinai; in contrast, "You have come to Mount Zion and to the city of the living God, the heavenly Jerusalem, and to innumerable angels in festal gathering, and to the assembly of the first-born who are enrolled in heaven, and to God the judge of all, and to the spirits of the righteous made perfect, and to Jesus the mediator of a new covenant, and to the sprinkled blood that speaks a better word than the blood of Abel" (vv. 22-24). These verses summarize the whole theology of Hebrews, whose view of the final consummation a quotation from Haggai introduces: "'Yet once more I will shake not only the earth but also the heaven.' This phrase, 'Yet once more,' indicates the removal of what is shaken — that is, of created things — so that what cannot be shaken may remain. Therefore, since we are receiving a kingdom that cannot be shaken, let us give thanks, by which we offer to God an acceptable worship with reverence and awe; for indeed our God is a consuming fire" (12:26-29).

The interplay between theology and exhortation in Hebrews is an excellent example of the relationship of faith and behavior in Christianity, whose moral code is the natural consequence of the saving act of God in the incarnation, death, and resurrection of the Son.

5

Response to the Light: John

The Fourth Gospel, whose author or authors we shall simply call "John," is sometimes called the "spiritual Gospel." It contains the narrative of Jesus' miracles, controversies, death, and resurrection in common with the other three, but differs insofar as in it the words of Jesus, unlike the Synoptic sayings, are presented as long discourses, couched in symbolical language approaching that of mysticism, similar in style to John's first epistle. Symbolical terms are polyvalent, hard to pin down to definite meanings even in the context of their use elsewhere in the whole Bible. They are the subject of prayerful meditation rather than of philological analysis; nonetheless, to dissociate their interpretation from strict exegesis may lead to flights of fancy not based on Scripture.

Another difficulty in interpreting John's Gospel is that it has to be read on three intertwining levels: that of factual history, that of the exalted Christ, and that of the controversies of the Johannine community with the synagogue. John's Christology, moreover, begins where that of the Synoptics ends; in the latter Jesus was condemned for claiming to be the Christ the Son of God, whereas in John he often speaks of being equal to and one with the Father, defining himself simply as "I am," and this results in his condemnation.

There is a clear dualism in the writings of John: light as opposed to darkness, life to death, from above to from below, flesh to spirit, truth to deceit, "the world" to the believers, blindness to faith. This brings it close to the theology of Qumran and some contemporary Hellenistic writings, which broadens its hermeneutical context. "Johannine spirituality," therefore, is an evasive concept, brilliantly dealt with by Origen and Augustine, but requiring further elucidation in the light of modern exegesis. Our synthetic view will limit itself to presenting some typical themes in the Gospel and in 1 John to help the reader to delve deeper into these unfathomable concepts.

The Word of Life

John's prologue presents Jesus Christ as the Word, Logos, made flesh, to provide the reader with a pre-understanding of all that is to follow. "In the beginning was the Word, and the Word was with God, and the Word was God" (1:1). Human words are audible sounds that reveal the speaker's invisible thoughts, sentiments, moods, power, and personality. *Logos* in Greek also means reason, hence the word "logic," but in Hellenistic Judaism it stood for God's wisdom through which he created the world, while in Stoic philosophy it denoted the immanent intelligent factor that gave rationality to the universe. By calling the pre-incarnate Christ "Word," therefore, John deliberately triggers several connotations within the minds of his readers, who came from both Judaism and the Hellenistic world. The novelty of the prologue, however, is that, while in Judaism the "word" was a synonym for "wisdom," the personification of an attribute of God, and in philosophy an impersonal *anima mundi*, in John it is a person who took on flesh in Jesus, revealing God's true face: "No one has ever seen God. It is God the only Son, who is close to the Father's heart, who has made him known" (1:18); "Whoever has seen me has seen the Father" (14:9).

"In him (i.e., in the Word) was life, and the life was the light of all people" (1:4). Life is the fullness of being and of existence, which is God's essence, communicated to the Word; its splendor shines on human beings, opening their eyes to the Truth, to God himself. The refusal of light, of revelation, is the refusal of life itself, leaving people in the darkness of "the world," a darkness that leads to death. "The light shines in the darkness, and the darkness did not overcome it" (1:5) because this radiance contains the power of life. Life and truth can be crucified because "the world did not know him" (1:10), but they cannot be extinguished, for God's life-giving power overcomes death itself. "But to all who received him, who believed in his name, he gave power to become children of God, who were born, not of blood or of the will of the flesh or of the will of man, but of God" (1:12-13). What the Only-begotten received from the Father will now be shared by those who believe; they are born into a higher existence and acquire a new personality embodied in Christ's Sonship and sharing the dynamism of God's life.

"And the Word became flesh and lived among us . . . full of grace and truth" (1:14). This can be paraphrased as "the Word became a human being, with all his physical and psychological limitations; he sojourned among us as would a stranger, but he brought with him the fullness of the Father's love and the reality of all that had been foreshadowed in previous revelation." Grace and truth can be a hendiadys just meaning the gift of truth, or the true grace in contrast with the shadowy insufficiency of God's self-disclosure in the Old Testament. In fact, "the law indeed was given through Moses; grace and truth came through Jesus Christ" (1:17).

The prologue is often likened to the overture of one of Wagner's operas, which contains the main musical keynotes that will be developed later into arias by the various personages to characterize them. It is to some of these arias that we now turn our attention.

Reading the Signs

We have already said that John calls Jesus' miracles "signs," that is, they are not an end to themselves, they are not merely acts of beneficence, they point to something beyond themselves and must be read in that key if they are to mean something. St. Augustine likens miracles to a beautifully written manuscript shown to one who cannot read; he may admire the beauty of the letters but they convey no meaning to him.

John introduces Jesus' public ministry with the Baptist's witness: "Here is the Lamb of God, who takes away the sin of the world! This is he of whom I said, 'After me comes a man who ranks ahead of me because he was before me'" (1:29). John testifies that he saw the Spirit descending upon Jesus in his baptism, meaning that Jesus was to baptize with the Spirit and not with water alone. John deduces from this that Jesus is the Son of God (1:32-34). The epithet "Lamb of God" recalls the paschal lamb as well as the Suffering Servant in Isaiah 53:7. So does the mention of the Spirit descending upon Jesus (Isa. 42:1); but the Baptist goes further, he proclaims Jesus' Sonship in the sense of the pre-existence of the Word.

Two of John's disciples accept his testimony and follow Jesus. They ask him with all simplicity, "Where are you staying?," meaning "Where do you live?" The answer is "Come and see." He cannot give them his address because his abode is in heaven with the Father, but only those who "spend a day" with him, that is, who undergo the experience of his fellowship, will understand this. The evangelist indicates the time of this encounter and in the course of his narrative he often scans the hour until the "supreme hour" arrives, thus inviting the reader to spend "a day" meditating on his

Gospel to arrive at the perception of where Jesus really abides (1:35-39).

These two disciples immediately spread the word and verses 41-51 contain some confessions of faith following a simple meeting with Jesus: "We have found the Messiah" (v. 41); "We have found him about whom Moses in the law and also the prophets wrote, Jesus son of Joseph from Nazareth" (v. 45); "Rabbi, you are the Son of God! You are the King of Israel!" (v. 49).

The first real "sign" Jesus performs is the conversion of water into wine at Cana (2:1-11), in which he manifests his glory, and his disciples believe in him. This well-known narrative has been a *crux interpretum* for centuries; we shall comment on it briefly in line with a number of modern exegetes. Changing water to wine would be quite a useless miracle if it did not have a deeper meaning; the details of the narrative contain a key to its interpretation. The setting is a wedding, in which probably the whole village took part, and thus an occasion of joy, marred only by the lack of wine as the feast proceeds. John makes no other mention of weddings or spouses. In Matthew 9:15 we find a reference to Jesus as bridegroom, and in Ephesians 5:32 as well as in Revelation 21 to the church as the bride of Christ. Does the evangelist mean to drop a hint that it was Jesus who was the real spouse? In this second chapter, John also introduces the "mother of Jesus" for the first time. It is she who notices the embarrassment of the couple because of the lack of wine, and puts her son into the picture with all simplicity. Did it imply a request for help in whatever way? Jesus' answer comes as a surprise: "Woman, what concern is that to you and to me? My hour has not yet come" (v. 4), and Mary's response is no less surprising when she tells the servants to do whatever Jesus tells them. As in many parables the lack of logic in the narration points to the assumption that the logic "from above" does not follow the course of a rationality "from below." First of all the appellative "Woman" is strange; why not "Mother"? We find the same address in John 19:26 when Jesus' hour to be "lifted up" had come, and this common usage links the two episodes together. The remark that the six big water jars served "for the Jewish rites of purification" (v. 6) is essential for the interpretation of the whole episode; they symbolize the purification rites of the Old Testament, which Jesus will convert into the exquisite wine of the New; not now, however, but when his hour comes, the time to be lifted up on the cross and to the Father. It is then that Jesus' symbolic miracle at Cana will find its true actualization. It is also then that he will appoint his mother as mother of the beloved disciple and of the whole church. The observation that no one knew where this good wine came from except the *diakonoi*, the servants (v. 9), will point to his disciples who will one day dispense the wine of the New Testament to all who participate in the nuptials of the Lamb with his heavenly spouse (cf. Rev. 21:9-11). After seeing this sign, "his disciples believed in him" (v. 11).

The next sign, not a miraculous one, is the cleansing of the temple, on which occasion Jesus proclaims, "Destroy this temple, and in three days I will raise it up" (2:19), meaning, as John comments, the temple of Jesus' body (2:21). This saying, according to the Synoptics, was cited against him at the trial and provided the occasion for his condemnation. However, the narrative continues, during Passover many believed in his name on seeing his miracles, but Jesus "would not entrust himself to them, because he knew all people and needed no one to testify about anyone; for he himself knew what was in everyone" (2:23-25).

Perhaps one of them was Nicodemus, whose visit to Jesus is recounted in 3:1-15. He came "by night" because his mind was still darkened; he had seen Jesus' signs with marvel, but he could not "read" them, and it was only later that he would see the light. The conversation between Jesus and this member of the Sanhedrin is a paradigm of similar discussions which the Johannine community had with well-meaning Jews who were attracted to Christianity and wondered at the charisms and miracles in its midst. The substance of Jesus' and the community's message is that good intentions are not sufficient; to enter the kingdom of God baptism is necessary, and not merely the purifications of the Jews or the Baptist's ritual, but Jesus' baptism, which confers the Holy Spirit, the essence of new covenant status; it regenerates the person so that he or she now belongs to the world "from above." The Son of Man who descended "from above" was to be "lifted up," first on the cross, then in heaven, and faith in him would transfer also the believer into this higher existence. Apart from baptism with the Spirit, the neophyte must accept the Johannine kerygma, summarized in verses 16-21, 31-36, and in 1 John 4:7-10: The presence of the Son is a sign of the Father's love for the world; he is here as savior, not as judge. Condemnation is an auto-judgment of those who refuse to believe in the light because they prefer the evil works of darkness. We can refer again here to St. Augustine, who says that afflicted eyes hate that very light which healthy eyes love so dearly. Jesus comes from above and speaks what he has heard from God, who is love; to believe his words therefore is to receive life eternal, which the Spirit communicates without measure. The First Letter of John adds that God's love manifests itself in the sending of the Son as an expiation for our sins. This is what Jesus' signs actually mean: whoever can read them with clear eyes responds with a confession of faith that corresponds to John's preaching.

The process of the response of faith to Jesus' self-manifestation by means of signs can be studied in his meeting with the Samaritan woman at the well (4:1-42). In the course of the conversation we find once more the comparison between the water from Jacob's well and the living water of eternal life Christ gives. The dialogue is typically Johannine; Jesus talks of heavenly things, things from above, but the interlocutor understands them in an earthly manner, from below. The sign Jesus gives is that of telling this unknown woman all about her past life; he then goes on to tell her that the cult of the new covenant will not be a local temple cult but a cult of worship "in Spirit and in truth," in his own body, as seen above. He finally proclaims himself as the Messiah *(taeb)* expected by both Jews and Samaritans (4:26). In response the woman first treats him with contempt as a Jew; her address changes later to "sir," and when Jesus has read her heart and revealed her hidden life she, though yet immature, acknowledges him as "a prophet." She announces him to her people as the possible Messiah, and the story ends with their confession that this is truly "the Savior of the world." This time the light has shone in the darkness and illuminated it fully.

The exact opposite happens in the healing of the man born blind in chapter 9. This is not only a prodigious miracle, it is a sign that, if rightly read with its rich typology, illustrates both Jesus' person and his mission. The whole issue is the blindness of the Pharisees who do their best to deny or explain away the fact that has become known all over. The typology of the narrative recalls the theology contained in the Nicodemus episode. The blind man is anointed; he is told to wash his eyes in the fountain of Siloam, interpreted "Sent," to mean baptism in the "Sent One" who is Christ (v. 7). In early Christianity, baptism was called *photismós*, illumination. We can observe the process of spiritual illumination in the man who was healed. He first refers to Jesus as "the man called Jesus" (v. 11), then proclaims him as a prophet (v. 17), for which he is expelled from the synagogue, and ends up by confessing Jesus as the Son of Man (vv. 35-38). We observed a similar process of illumination in the Samaritan woman. Acknowledging Jesus as a prophet is positive in John's view, but it is not sufficient. Jesus is much more than a prophet of old; he is the Son of Man, the Savior of the world, the Son of God, and must be confessed as such. The process of illumination is in sharp contrast with the blinding of the Pharisees. Jesus proclaimed in 8:12: "I am the light of the world." Now he says: "'I came into this world for judgment so that those who do not see may see, and those who do see may become blind.' Some of the Pharisees near him heard this and said to him, 'Surely we are not blind, are we?' Jesus said to them, 'If you were blind, you would not have sin. But now that you say, "We see," your sin remains'" (vv. 39-41).

We find the last example of the contrast between belief and blindness in the episode of the raising of Lazarus in chapter 11, which foreshadows Jesus' own resurrection. The miracle is preceded by the "I am" saying: "I am the resurrection and the life. Those who believe in me, even though they die, will live, and everyone who lives and believes in me will never die" (11:25), followed by Martha's confession: "I believe that you are the Messiah, the Son of God, the one coming into the world" (v. 27). As the fact is so obvious that only the blind can deny it, the Pharisees decide to kill Lazarus to wipe away the evidence, as if (again Augustine) he who raised himself from the dead could not raise again a murdered Lazarus. No wonder then that the first part of the Gospel ends with a quotation from Isaiah 6:10: "He has blinded their eyes and hardened their heart, so that they might not look with their eyes, and understand with their heart and turn — and I would heal them" (12:40).

The Bread of Life

In chapter 6, John takes up the accounts of the multiplying of loaves found in Mark 6:32-44 and 8:1-10. As usual we hear Jesus' proclamation: "I am the bread of life. Whoever comes to me will never be hungry, and whoever believes in me will never be thirsty" (v. 35). This time the simple people who witness the miracle want to "make him king" (v. 15), but Jesus, knowing that his kingship "is not from this world" (18:36), goes up to a mountain to pray for the disciples in distress in the stormy lake, in the same way he will later ascend into heaven to intercede for his church. The long discourse on

Christ being the bread of life descended from heaven recalls the manna in the desert but stands in contrast to it, as the manna was only material bread and those who ate it eventually died. Eating, in the sense of believing in Jesus, will give eternal life and immortality (vv. 49-51). In the Old Testament, Wisdom invites all to partake of her life-giving power (Sir. 24:19-21). Jesus is Wisdom itself become flesh, and it is Jesus' flesh that must now be eaten (v. 51). Not all understand this, only those who are taught by God (vv. 41ff.; see Isa. 54:13; Jer. 31:34). Indeed, it is not only "the Jews" who are scandalized by this saying but also some of the disciples themselves, who "turned back and no longer went about with him" (v. 66), symbolized by Judas's defection (v. 71), also an allusion to the Docetists who will later deny the reality of Jesus' body (1 John 4:2; 2 John 7). To prevent any anthropophagical interpretation John adds the explanation that the flesh Jesus is speaking of is the flesh of the risen Christ, the Son of Man ascended to heaven where he belongs (v. 62), but it is only by means of the illumination of the Holy Spirit that this teaching can be apprehended (v. 63). In fact, when asked if they too want to leave Jesus, the twelve answer through Peter, taught by the Father: "Lord, to whom can we go? You have the words of eternal life. We have come to believe and know that you are the Holy One of God" (vv. 68-69).

We have explored the meaning of the Eucharist in a previous chapter. Here suffice it to say that John repeats in his own terminology the essentials of the doctrine we find in the Synoptics and in Paul: we find "flesh" instead of "body"; "for the life of the world" replaces "given up for you," the eternal life promised to all who eat his flesh and drink his blood corresponds to Paul's eschatological view.

I and the Father Are One

We have observed that each of John's signs is followed by an "I am" saying and a confession of faith as response. Jesus' greatest sign is obviously his resurrection; it is to this event that he pointed when asked after the cleansing of the temple: "What sign can you show us for doing this?" (2:18). His answer was the raising of his body on the third day. It is therefore clear that the highest confession of faith we find in the Gospel is Thomas's declaration, "My Lord and my God!" (20:28). The proclamation of Jesus as prophet, Messiah, Son of Man, Son of God, King, and Savior of the world were certainly acceptable to and approved by him, but what distinguishes John's Christology is that Jesus, the Word made flesh, is God. In the Synoptics we find a hint to this claim in Jesus' trial. The admission that he was the Son of God provoked his condemnation for blasphemy, meaning that the Sanhedrin had understood the implications of such a claim perhaps even better than the disciples themselves. John does not report this trial at the end of Jesus' ministry; he only narrates the trial before Pilate, who finds Jesus innocent, but the whole of the Fourth Gospel is a trial scene, especially chapters 5, 7, 8, and 10. The final condemnation is to be found in 11:47-53, following Caiaphas's prophetic declaration that "it is better for you to have one man die for the people than to have the whole nation destroyed."

In John 5 we have a long discourse by Jesus in answer to the accusation of the Jews that he had cured a man at the pool of Bethzatha on the sabbath. He introduces it by the statement: "My Father is still working, and I also am working" (v. 17), which provokes the serious accusation that he is making himself equal to God. The narrative of this miracle is already symbolical: the five porticos of the pool, under which lay a multitude of invalids, recall the Pentateuch. Jesus develops three main points in his response: the operative unity of himself and the Father (vv. 19-24); the fullness of life he received from the Father to be granted to humankind (vv. 25-30); his witness is God (vv. 31-38). The logic of these three arguments is a complete answer to the accusation that healing on a sabbath is not God's work. The Father is always at work, so is the Son. The healing of an invalid is a sign of Jesus' life-giving power; God renders witness to Jesus through his miracles.

The Father, with whom the Son is united in perfect love, has placed both life-giving power and judgment in the Son's hands: the Son can raise the dead as the Father can, and he has the power of judgment, so that honor to God cannot be dissociated from honor to the Son. Refusal of faith in the Son means condemnation, whereas belief leads to eternal life. The resurrection of the dead is a consequence of the fullness of life the Son received from the Father. Jesus is not only the Son of God; he is also the Son of Man of whom Daniel (7:13-14) spoke. Hence he is able to judge, but his judgment is in accordance with that of the Father. Lastly, Jesus does not render witness to himself; the Baptist had already testified about him. Rather, it is his miracles that render witness, as do the Scriptures. If one has understood Moses rightly and one attunes one's ear to God's voice one will immediately recognize this voice in Jesus' words and deeds.

In chapter 7 Jesus' discourse in the temple at the feast of tabernacles continues that of chapter 5 as if the intervening chapter 6 were absent. He accuses the Jews that they do not observe the law of Moses and do not know God. This causes dissent among the crowd; some begin to doubt, and others say he is a madman. He cannot be the Messiah, they insist, for he does not come from Bethlehem, thus showing — according to John — that they know neither Jesus' divine nor his human origin. In verses 33-39 Christ foretells his return to heaven, whence he descended, and the sending of the Holy Spirit on those who believe in him. Once more he is met with skepticism and unbelief from the Jewish officials.

It is in the next chapter, however, that Jesus' claim to divinity reaches its climax. In relating the controversy discourses with the Jews, John follows his usual spiral-movement style, repeating themes from the preceding chapter but at a higher level. Jesus begins by proclaiming himself as the light of the world (8:12). In answer to the charge that he is bearing witness to himself, he says: "Even if I testify on my own behalf, my testimony is valid because I know where I have come from and where I am going. . . . I testify on my own behalf, and the Father who sent me testifies on my behalf. . . . You know neither me nor my Father. If you knew me, you would know my Father also" (8:14, 18, 19). Their ignorance is due to the fact that "You are from below, I am from above; you are of this world, I am not of this world" (v. 23). Jesus here introduces his self-definition as the absolute "I am," without any predicate, with reference to Yahweh's "I AM WHO I AM" in Exodus 3:14; but this will only be evident when he is lifted up, first on the cross, then to heaven where he belongs (v. 28). A controversy about Abraham follows, ending in the supreme saying: "Very truly, I tell you, before Abraham was, I am" (v. 58). It is the I AM of divine pre-existence and of eternity. "So they picked up stones to throw at him, but Jesus hid himself and went out of the temple" (v. 59). As at Cana, his "hour" had not yet come.

The Self-revelation to the Disciples

The five chapters preceding John's passion narrative replace the account of the Last Supper in the Synoptics. They are usually called the farewell discourses and belong to a literary genre often found in the Bible. Jesus opens his heart to his disciples to deepen their faith and prepare them for their mission.

"Now before the festival of the Passover, Jesus knew that his hour had come to depart from this world and go to the Father. Having loved his own who were in the world, he loved them to the end"

(13:1). This solemn opening introduces Jesus' washing of the disciples' feet. Washing the feet was usually a slave's task and this is precisely why Jesus took it upon himself: "Do you know what I have done to you? You call me Teacher and Lord — and you are right, for that is what I am. So if I, your Lord and Teacher, have washed your feet, you also ought to wash one another's feet" (13:12-14). It is a lesson in humility and mutual service.

An episode that casts a shadow on this gathering is Jesus' foretelling of Judas's betrayal. For John, Judas becomes the prototype of all who abandon their belief in Christ. The morsel Jesus gives Judas to eat, an act of love but also a warning, drives Satan into him, who then leads him into the night of "the world," where he will find death instead of eternal life. The oft-repeated command to "remain in me" in John's Gospel is an exhortation to all believers not to relinquish their steadfast faith in Jesus and fall back into the darkness of a world dominated by the evil one (13:21-30). Nonetheless Jesus can forgive Peter's triple denial, for it is due to Peter's weakness rather than his lack of love (vv. 36-38).

When Judas departs, Jesus announces the mutual glorification of the Son of Man and of God, as well as his return to the Father. He leaves them as testament the "new commandment" to love one another as he loved them. The newness of this commandment lies in the manner love is conceived; it is the "love to the end" of 13:1, to lay down their lives for one another; it will be the distinctive sign of true discipleship to the whole world (v. 35).

Jesus returns to the Father to prepare the way for the disciples' own return. His answer to Thomas's bafflement on where he is going, "I am the way, and the truth, and the life. No one comes to the Father except through me" (14:6), is a clear statement that Christ is the only Mediator between God and humankind; he is the personified truth of the Father's love, for "in him was life, and the life was the light of all people" (1:4). His revelation is the brilliance emanating from the life-giving power of God's life itself. Consequently,

Philip's ingenuous request, "Lord, show us the Father, and we will be satisfied" (14:8-10), can only have one answer: "Whoever has seen me has seen the Father. . . . I am in the Father and the Father is in me." "Seeing" here implies that firm belief in Jesus that perceives the splendor of divinity shining through his humanity and can confess: "We have seen his glory, the glory as of a father's only son" (1:14). Would this refer to that transfiguration in Mark 9:2-8?

Faith-perception is made possible by the Holy Spirit to whom various passages refer in these chapters: 14:16-17; 15:26-27; 16:7-15. John calls the Spirit "*Parakletos*," a term difficult to translate with a single word; it is sometimes translated as "counselor," at other times as "consoler" or "advocate." In reality, as the etymology of the word suggests, the *parakletos* was a friend who stood by you in a trial or in your tribulations to advise you and defend your cause as well as to offer solace. When Jesus speaks of "another *parakletos*" he implies that he himself is one insofar as he intercedes for us with the Father, illuminates, and consoles us. We shall link the passages on the Spirit with each other to synthesize their message, which holds a central place in Johannine teaching and spirituality.

The Spirit is given by the Father through Jesus' intercession, and will remain with the church forever. He is the Spirit of truth because he is a constant source of recollection of the teaching of Jesus, who is the truth. It is only those who love Jesus and observe his commandment to believe in him and to love one another who can perceive the presence of the Spirit; the world is not able to do so because of its blindness in faith. As the Spirit proceeds from the Father, who bears witness to Jesus, he too will bear witness to him and will help all believers to do the same. He will come into the world when Jesus has been exalted to heaven, for it is the risen Christ who will send the Spirit to continue his presence among his believers in history. The world had condemned Christ; now it is its turn to be condemned by him through the Spirit, who will act as prosecuting attorney to accuse it of its lack of belief in Jesus and of the injustice committed in Jesus' condemnation to death, now witnessed by God who has raised him to heaven, and to pronounce the final condemnation on Satan, source of the wickedness and blindness of "the world," whose ruler Satan is. Within the church, however, the Spirit will not only continue but even develop Jesus' teaching, accommodating it to the needs of the age, and endowing believers with the spirit of prophecy. As Christ is all that the Father is, whatever the Spirit reveals is the revelation of both Father and Son. This is the manner in which the *Parakletos* will glorify the Christ.

Although the Spirit, like the wind, "blows where it chooses" (3:8), it is received by those who not only believe, but remain in Christ. John translates the Pauline metaphor of the (mystical) body of Christ into that of vine and branches (15:1-11). Jesus is the vine; the branches are those who believe in him. They cannot bear the fruit of works of love of themselves; it is only by their union with the vine that they can do so. If they cut themselves off they will wither and become only material for burning. Remaining in Jesus requires the observance of his commandments; if believers follow Jesus' teaching with sincerity, they can ask anything of God and it will be given them because of the Father's love of Jesus. Those who believe have been chosen by Christ and thus are no longer servants but friends (15:14-15). For this they will be hated by that same world that hated Jesus and the Father; they will consequently suffer the same fate he suffered (15:18-25).

Eternal Life

Where does the light of faith lead? John's eschatology is often called "realized eschatology"; that is, the blessings of eternal life, which "consequent eschatology" places in the hereafter, are already present in the believer. Jesus' presence in the world is already a criterion for judgment on those who do not accept him, and of life eternal for whoever believes. Yet we have seen that Jesus does indeed speak of the resurrection and of the dead rising from their tombs for reward or punishment (5:28-29), but that as he himself is "the resurrection and the life," "those who believe in me, even though they die, will live, and everyone who lives and believes in me will never die" (11:25-26). In chapter 16, however, Jesus speaks of his return, which can refer either to the apparitions after the resurrection or to his final return (16:19). There is no spectacular scene of judgment in John as we find in Matthew 24 or in Mark 13. We pass judgment upon ourselves by accepting or rejecting Christ; we receive the reward or punishment of God's life or of separation from God in our own lives, a judgment that will be authenticated in the resurrection.

Life and death in biblical usage have various meanings. Life means biological life, but it also denotes union with God the source of life, as well as life in the hereafter. Death too has these three levels of meaning: physical death, separation from God, and eschatological death, which the Apocalypse calls "the second death" (Rev. 2:11); but it also denotes a cosmic destructive power that dominates humankind. It is the last enemy to be destroyed by Christ (1 Cor. 15:26; Rev. 20:14; 21:4). Eternal life is not merely a life of immortality in the world to come; it is qualitative rather than quantitative, a participation of God's own life with the beatitude to which we all aspire. As Christ possessed life in its fullness, so also he communicates it to the believer both in this world and in the resurrection.

Christ's Intercessory Prayer

Jesus' discourse to his disciples ends with the so-called priestly prayer in chapter 17. This is a curious composition and presents Jesus as it were hovering between heaven and earth. It certainly corresponds with the concept John and his community had of the heavenly intercession of the risen Christ, based on his earthly sayings and prayers. I present its main points in paraphrase. "The hour" which is so often anticipated in this Gospel has now arrived: Jesus will be "exalted," first on the cross and then to heaven, what we call the "paschal mystery," through which the Father glorifies the Son as he is glorified by the Son's obedience in his mission. Glorification means the power given to Christ over humankind (cf. Matt. 28:18); it is the communication of that life the Logos had from eternity to those the Father chooses and hands over to Christ. Now Jesus has completed his mission. For his obedience he will be raised to that glory, honor, and power he had in his pre-existence (cf. Phil. 2:9-11). His assignment had been that of revealing the true nature of the Father to the chosen ones, so that they may be convinced of the intimate union between Father and Son and the identity of their revelation. Christ does not pray for the world, but for those his Father has given him and who have believed, or will believe in him through their word. That is, his intercession does not profit those who refuse to believe ("the world" in its negative sense). On the other hand, he has come to save the world, those who are open to his message. While Christ is now in heaven the disciples are still in the world. Christ therefore begs the Father to "protect them" in God's name, that is, by the power of his grace. The supreme gift Jesus asks for them is that of unity, modeled on his own unity with the Father. He had preserved his disciples while he was with them; now he entrusts them to his Father. Because they are not "of the world," but live in the world, "the world" hates them as it hated Jesus. Jesus' request is not that they be removed from the world but that they may be defended from the Evil One who is the "ruler of this world." May they be sanctified in the truth, which will consecrate them to God, as Jesus himself is now offering himself to the Father in his last hour. God's word (or Word) is truth. Believers of all ages will be endowed with that same power of grace Christ received from the Father, and will share their unity. It is this unity that should witness to the world that God sent Jesus, and that they participate in the love between Father and Son. The purpose of this prayer is that they may one day come to contemplate Christ's glory, which he had with the Father before the creation itself. His mission was to reveal God's true face; he has completed it and now he desires that the love between himself and the Father may embrace all those who believe in him.

The First Epistle of John

In the above prayer Jesus says: "While I was with them, I protected them in your name that you have given me. I guarded them, and not one of them was lost except the one destined to be lost, so that the scripture might be fulfilled" (John 17:12). The one destined to be lost is of course Judas Iscariot, who, we have already said, is the prototype of all "who no longer went about with Jesus" (John 6:66). What happened during Jesus' ministry will also happen after his departure. There will always be those "destined to be lost" who swerve away from that unity Christ so ardently desires. The First Letter of John is a witness to the birth of schism. It seems to have been prompted by some who stressed Christ's divinity so rigidly that they began to question the reality of his humanity; it is what will later be called "docetism," which held that Jesus' body was merely apparent, not a material one like ours. So while the prologue to John's Gospel was all about the pre-existence of the Word and his oneness with God, the prologue to 1 John, though still calling Jesus the "word of life" (1:1), stresses the fact that the writer and other witnesses had actually seen, heard, and touched Christ.

John opens with the apparently obvious statement that the message he had received from Christ and preached to all is that

God is light, and that there is no darkness in him (1:5). This is essential to the Johannine kerygma. Light is the transparency of God's righteousness and holiness; therefore whoever walks in the darkness of sin cannot claim to be in union with God. The community is on the brink of a schism, as later events, reported in 2 and 3 John, show. If unity and love are to be maintained, believers must adhere firmly to John's initial preaching, which is the foundation and backbone of their faith; swerving away from it leads to darkness, away from God and Christ. Paul had drawn the same conclusion in 1 Corinthians 15, and both Paul's kerygma and John's flowed into our creed, which professes the death and resurrection of Jesus, as well as the confession that he is "light from light."

Another definition of God, repeated twice in this letter, is that God is love (4:8, 16); as the one who does not walk in the light is not from God, so the one who does not love does not know God: "God's love was revealed among us in this way: God sent his only Son into the world so that we might live through him. In this is love, not that we loved God but that he loved us and sent his Son to be the atoning sacrifice for our sins. Beloved, since God loved us so much, we also ought to love one another. No one has ever seen God; if we love one another, God lives in us, and his love is perfected in us" (4:9-12). Disruption in the community is sin, and those who cause it must acknowledge it; they lie to themselves if they think they have fellowship with God. If they do confess this fault, however, the blood of Jesus Christ will wash all iniquity from them (1:6-9). In fact, these people are playing the part of the antichrist who is coming; they left the community, but they were never truly part of it, otherwise they would have maintained unity (2:18-19). Now as for the believers who may still be in doubt, the anointing by the Holy One, in the spirit of Jeremiah 31:33-34, will be their interior teacher to keep them in the truth (2:20, 27-28). They must also beware of those who claim to have the spirit of prophecy but are actually false prophets. No true prophet can contradict the kerygma that was from the beginning: "By this you know the Spirit of God: every spirit that confesses that Jesus Christ has come in the flesh is from God, and every spirit that does not confess Jesus is not from God. And this is the spirit of the antichrist, of which you have heard that it is coming; and now it is already in the world" (4:2-3). The secessionists belong to "the world" and that is the reason why their teaching is welcomed by it. On the contrary those who remain firm in the faith and listen to John's teaching are of God (4:4-6). God renders witness to the truth of the doctrine they received through the sacraments of water, blood, and Spirit, perhaps a reference to the sacraments of baptism, Eucharist, and anointing (5:6-9).

The spirit of John's first letter, therefore, is that of translating Jesus' farewell discourses into practice within the ecclesial community. "The world" has permeated the church itself, and belonging to it or to Christ can only be verified by adherence to the apostolic teaching and the maintenance of the bond of love. It is in light of this criterion that we must read the subsequent history of schism and heresy in the church. The faith of the main body of the church is animated by the Spirit and moves forward with its own pace in the course of history: progressives (cf. *proagon* in 2 John 9) who run too far ahead, and traditionalists who never catch up with others, are both out of step. A meditation on the theology of history in the spirit of John's letters can be of great help to the ecumenical movement.

We can reduce to quite a simple formula the substance of Johannine spirituality, whether in the Gospel or in the epistles. It is the response, by the help of the Spirit, to the Father's love in sending the Logos-Son into the world, in real flesh, to bring the light of revelation to all so that all may know God's true nature in the person, words, and deeds of Jesus Christ. One can either receive this light and obtain life, or be blinded by it through pride and remain "in the world." Remaining or persevering in the light of truth and in the love of God and neighbor means walking in the only way to God, in Christ. Leaving the warmth and light of the Upper Room, like Judas, is a return to the cold and darkness of "the world." Adherence to Christ is the source of life in this world and of resurrection in the next.

6

Response to Christ's Presence in History: Acts and Revelation

L et us recall some sayings of Jesus:

"Go therefore and make disciples of all nations, baptizing them in the name of the Father and of the Son and of the Holy Spirit, and teaching them to obey everything that I have commanded you. And remember, I am with you always, to the end of the age" (Matt. 28:19-20).

"Many will come in my name and say, 'I am he!' and they will lead many astray. When you hear of wars and rumors of wars, do not be alarmed; this must take place, but the end is still to come. For nation will rise against nation, and kingdom against kingdom; there will be earthquakes in various places; there will be famines. This is but the beginning of the birthpangs. As for yourselves, beware; for they will hand you over to councils; and you will be beaten in synagogues; and you will stand before governors and kings because of me, as a testimony to them. And the good news must first be proclaimed to all nations" (Mark 13:6-10).

"But in those days, after that suffering, the sun will be darkened, and the moon will not give its light, and the stars will be falling from heaven, and the powers in the heavens will be shaken. Then they will see 'the Son of Man coming in clouds' with great power and glory. Then he will send out the angels, and gather his elect from the four winds, from the ends of the earth to the ends of heaven" (Mark 13:24-27).

With these and similar words Jesus launches the church into history. She, and each and every believer, has the responsibility to spread the gospel to all, to bear the sufferings and the cross of Christ, to ride the storms of the vicissitudes of history, to guard against false teachings, and to await the coming of the Lord for the consummation of the redemption he initiated on earth.

The Acts of the Apostles

In his second book, Luke describes how the church began to accomplish this mission. It is true that the church is composed of men and women, but the prime mover in her mission is the Holy Spirit. The book of Acts begins with Jesus' ascent to heaven and the consequent pouring of the Spirit upon the apostles (cf. John 16:7-11). Just as the main actor in Israel's history had been God, it is now the Spirit who will lead the spread of the gospel, especially in the delicate phase of its transition from the Jews to the Gentiles. In the episode of the Ethiopian eunuch who was in contact with a foreign queen (Acts 8:26-39) it is the Spirit who sends Philip to evangelize him, and who removes him when his mission is over. In 9:31 it is again the Spirit who increases the number of those who believe. He is the principal agent in the conversion of Cornelius in chapter 10. Saul and Barnabas are personally chosen and commissioned by the Spirit (13:2-3), who plots their journeys step by step, by means of commands and prohibitions, until Paul reaches Europe (16:6; see Rom. 15:19). The apex of the Spirit's guidance is reached at the Jerusalem Council, in which the decision is taken, and proclaimed in his name, that the Gentiles are not to be subjected to circumcision and Torah observance (15:28-29). We may add to these texts from

Acts many expressions from the Pauline corpus in which the Spirit is conceived as the one who endows the word with power to penetrate people's hearts and create faith (Eph. 3:16-17; Heb. 4:12ff.; 1 Thess. 1:5; 1 Cor. 2:4; 2 Cor. 3:3).

The kerygmatic speeches in Acts 2, 3, 5, and 10, addressed to the Jews, stress the fact that the prophecies of the Old Testament are being fulfilled in Jesus of Nazareth, whom "God has made . . . both Lord and Messiah, this Jesus whom you crucified" (2:36). The descent of the Spirit is the essential sign of this fulfillment; Acts establishes the principle *ubi Spiritus ibi salus,* wherever the Spirit manifests itself, there is salvation. The descent of the Spirit on Cornelius's household in Acts 10 was the determining sign for Peter to baptize these uncircumcised Gentiles, first fruits of the proclamation of the gospel to the pagans. The content of the discourses in Acts is the same as that we saw in our reading of Paul, the saving death and resurrection of Christ, which is the center of our credo.

The spread of the gospel from Jerusalem, through Judea, Samaria, Antioch, Asia Minor, Greece, and finally to Rome in no more than two or three decades was a sign that faith gave hope and serenity to people who could make little sense of the very purpose of existence or of events taking place around them. The first converts were Jews, who were expecting the fulfillment of the promises to Israel, but this caused conflicts with their co-religionists, often in the same family, who found it difficult to believe, and persecution ensued. In the first three centuries it was the Roman state that continued this persecution. The injunction to bear the cross was becoming a reality. It is interesting to note that whenever Luke relates the trial or condemnation of a Christian he often uses phrases found in Jesus' passion narrative, which leads us to conclude that he shared Paul's conviction that his own sufferings were the prolongation of Jesus' passion: "In my flesh I am completing what is lacking in Christ's affliction for the sake of his body, that is, the church" (Col. 1:24).

Suffering for Christ is endemic in the church. The First Letter of Peter describes the situation very clearly: "Beloved, do not be surprised at the fiery ordeal that is taking place among you to test you, as though something strange were happening to you. But rejoice insofar as you share Christ's sufferings, so that you may also be glad and shout for joy when his glory is revealed. If you are reviled for the name of Christ, you are blessed, because the spirit of glory, which is the spirit of God, is resting on you. . . . If any of you suffers as a Christian, do not consider it a disgrace but glorify God because you bear this name" (1 Pet. 4:12-16).

A church that proclaims a gospel that runs counter to worldly assumptions and passions, though giving hope to people who are seeking God, is bound to unnerve those whose treasures lie only in the present eon. A church that does not undergo suffering in some way or another is a church that is accommodating herself to the world and hence not fulfilling her mission.

Graver yet than external persecutions are troubles arising within the church itself. In the first century a conflict arose between Paul and Jewish Christians who still held fast to the necessity of observing the Torah for salvation and considered the apostle of the Gentiles a traitor to the Jewish ideal. Paul was persecuted during his lifetime, as we see from Galatians and 2 Corinthians, but even after his death a *damnatio memoriae* was imminent if Luke had not recorded his activity in Acts. This book is usually called Acts of the Apostles, but of other apostles we hear very little, except for Peter; over half of the book is about Paul and the success of his mission. It is probably this that saved both his memory and allowed the incorporation of his epistles into the canon. Jewish Christianity died within a couple of centuries and the church became Paul's Gentile church. On the other hand, Peter, whose mission was mainly towards the Jews, and Paul, the Gentile evangelizer, represent two facets of the ecclesial community, which merged together to produce what is often termed Catholicism, in the sense of an open universal church, not limited to one people or race, but in which the Jewish heredity remained essential, unless she had to give up the Old Testament totally, as Marcion did later.

However, Paul's doctrine was not without its dangers. Freedom from the law and the thesis that only faith and not good works justified sinners, could easily have been misunderstood to mean absolute freedom and libertinism, and it seems from James's letter that some believers did misinterpret Paul; that epistle stepped in to restore the balance. Second-century Gnostics aggravated the situation and the early Fathers had to overcome many difficulties to establish and maintain the orthodox tradition. Christ is still walking on the waves to come and save Peter's boat from wreckage.

In the Pastoral Epistles we see the church organizing herself by regulating her internal structures to face both false doctrine and persecution. Rules are laid down for the creation of bishop-presbyters and deacons. A few years later Ignatius of Antioch witnesses to a triple hierarchy of bishop, priest, and deacon. No human society can survive without laws and structures. Charisms still abounded in the early church, as they do today, but, as we saw in John's community (and see 1 Cor. 14), they can sometimes cause disorder and even schism. The Pastorals, written in Paul's name, 1 and 2 Peter, written in Peter's, and 1 John, written in John's, point to the veneration believers at the end of the first century had for those traditions that stemmed from one of the great apostles, which is why these writings were later incorporated into the canon.

The Book of Revelation

Apokalypsis in Greek means "revelation," hence this book is called the Apocalypse, or revelation, to a seer who calls himself John, exiled on the island of Patmos for his witness to Christ (1:1). The revelation comes from God, given through Jesus Christ and delivered to John by an angel. Though the book belongs to the apocalyptic genre it is styled as "prophecy" in 1:3, but it is at the same time a circular letter to the Asian churches.

Apocalypses flowered between the second century B.C. and the second Christian century A.D., especially in apocryphal literature. Some of these writings described tours of the heavenly regions, revealing their mysteries; others, usually called "historical apocalypses," were more concerned with the meaning of historical events, interpreted in the light of divine guidance and design. In the Old Testament we find traces of apocalyptic in passages in Isaiah, Ezekiel, and Zechariah. Daniel is completely apocalyptic. In the New Testament we find this genre in Mark 13, 2 Thessalonians, 2 Peter, and, of course, in Revelation. Apocalypses were often pseudonymous, dualistic, used symbolical language, and appeared in times of stress or persecution with the purpose of opening broader horizons of hope and courage to a disheartened community. If they spoke of the consummation of history and of the world, it was only to assure believers of God's final victory over evil and encourage them to persevere in their faith.

Our Apocalypse is a perfect specimen of this genre in its historical specificity.

The writing of this book is usually dated around A.D. 94, during the reign of Domitian, who is said to have claimed divinity for himself under the title *dominus et deus noster*, opposed by Thomas's confession "My Lord and my God" (John 20:28). Emperor worship entailed sacrificing to the emperor, common in Asia Minor, especially in Pergamum, in which, of course, Christians could not take part. This caused a conflict in the conscience of many believers, for many public ceremonies, even occasional meetings of the trade corporations to which many Christians belonged, were inaugurated with a sacrifice to the protector god or to the emperor. Lack of participation meant exclusion from the corporation or being branded disloyal citizens. Persecution ensued, and some members of the community had already suffered martyrdom, while others surrendered to some compromise or other.

The Apocalypse of John (was this a pseudonym or was it the John of the Gospel or of the epistles?) had the purpose of exhorting Christians to steadfastness in their faith and to uncompromising loyalty; they had to persevere even in the face of persecution, for the struggle was between Christ and the heavenly powers on one side and the Roman Empire with all its political, social, and economic power on the other. It was a conflict of opposing values and called for either-or decisions, for the final victory was surely that of the risen Christ and surrender or compromise meant exclusion from his kingdom. The situation is depicted in pure black and white, with no shades of gray in-between.

John makes use of the symbolic language in common with books belonging to the apocalyptic genre. The symbols are gleaned from the Old Testament and from contemporary events and myth, very much like recomposing the image of the Pantocrator in the apse of a Byzantine church by means of little colored stones or *tesserae* taken from other mosaics here and there. There are no explicit quotations from the Old Testament, but we find constant references to books such as Exodus, Isaiah, Ezekiel, Zechariah, and Daniel, which the author reread and reinterpreted in the light of the Christ event. These provide the main key to understanding the symbols, which interpenetrate in continuous transformation like images in a dream. It is John's way of writing dynamic theology.

The inaugural vision of Christ as the Danielic Son of Man, and the description of all his attributes in 1:7-20 acts as a prelude to the seven letters in chapters 2 and 3, to the churches of Ephesus, Smyrna, Pergamum, Thyatira, Sardis, Philadelphia, and Laodicea, which, even in the specificity of their historical circumstances, represent the universal church. Each one of these letters is in the form of a prophetic pronouncement in the name of the risen

Christ, qualified by one of his attributes described in chapter 1, and comes through the Spirit. Each community is partly praised, partly blamed, admonished, encouraged to persevere and given promises of salvation. The function of these prophetic letters is best defined in the words of 1 Peter 4:17: "For the time has come for judgment to begin with the household of God; if it begins with us, what will be the end for those who do not obey the gospel of God?" The Son of Man's judgment begins within history itself before it culminates in his second coming; Revelation is realized eschatology.

In the spectacular celestial liturgy in chapters 4 and 5, in which the description of God's throne, his majesty, and the solemnity of his adoration transcend every imagination, the risen Christ, described as "a Lamb standing as if it had been slaughtered, having seven horns and seven eyes, which are the seven spirits of God sent out into all the earth" (5:6), is commissioned to receive from God's hand the sealed book containing his inscrutable decrees which only the Lamb can probe and reveal. The Lamb now becomes the protagonist of the whole drama that unfolds itself in the Apocalypse (cf. 6:16-17; 7:10-17; 14:10; 21:9-10).

The opening of the seven seals (6:1–8:1), like the blowing of the seven trumpets (8:6–9:21; 10:7; 11:15) and the pouring of the seven bowls (16:1-21), has repercussions on humans, on history, and on the cosmos that often upset the readers of this book. The notion of a God who punishes humanity with plagues, wars, famines, and death is hard to reconcile with the image of a loving and forgiving Father. Of the negative events that plague humanity and the whole world many, like wars and revolutions, are brought about by ourselves; others, like famines, droughts, and earthquakes, are natural disasters. The apocalyptic plagues can be interpreted as signs of a cosmic unbalance due to humanity's self-distancing from God and as an indication of what would happen if God "left the world to itself"; they are a call to repentance. It is evident that these upheavals affect both the good and the wicked, but they are read in various ways by different kinds of people (cf. in this regard Jesus' saying in Luke 13:1-5); some do repent, but others "cursed the God of heaven because of their pain and sores, and they did not repent of their deeds" (16:11), thus perpetuating the moral disorder which is at the root of these events. Christ's judgment in history does not spare even believers themselves, for "if you are to be taken captive, into captivity you go; if you kill with the sword, with the sword you must killed. Here is a call for the endurance and faith of the saints" (13:10).

Yet the seer would not be content with this simple explanation. Wars, pestilence, and cosmic upheavals are what we can call "casualties" in the deadly struggle between kingdom and anti-kingdom. John unfolds this idea by means of two opposite and conflicting sets of symbols. The Holy Trinity — God, the seven spirits, and Jesus Christ — appears in the salutation in 1:4-5. This finds its opposite in the Satanic trinity consisting of the dragon (12:9), who communicates his power to the sea beast (13:1, 4) and the land beast (13:11), representing the devil, Rome, and her representatives in Asia. The Lord God is the one "who is and who was and who is to come" (Rev. 1:8); the beast "was and is not" (17:11). The stormy sea from which the beast rises is unlike the heavenly "sea of glass, like crystal" (4:6). The Spirit is opposed to the false prophet (19:20). Michael's name, which means "Who is like God?" is mimicked by "Who is like the beast?" in 13:4. Babylon (18:9) is the negative counterpart of Jerusalem, while the woman in 12:1 is counteracted by the whore (17:1). Michael's angels battle against the demonic angels in 12:7, and the scarlet antichrist of 17:3 opposes Christ. These oppositions are not accidental but are a literary device upon which the writer meditated deeply.

What do these symbols tell us? John lived in the oppressive society of the Roman Empire; Christians found themselves ill at ease religiously, politically, socially, and economically. By translating a definite historical situation into symbols John abstracted its essence and rendered it applicable to all similar situations in all times and places. In algebra letters are symbols that can represent any number and an algebraic formula is applicable to any set of numbers. By reducing definite events and circumstances to a symbolic formula, John's book speaks always and everywhere. The spirituality of the Apocalypse is applicable today in countries with politically or economically oppressive structures in which the Christian must either surrender his evangelical values or suffer persecution in some way or other. Whereas apocalyptic tends to depict situations in black and white, in reality empires and governments are not always opposed to Christian values. In fact, in Romans 13:1-7 Paul exhorts everyone to be subject to the governing authorities, for every authority comes from God. Christians therefore must be good citizens and they shall have nothing to fear. Rulers are there to keep law and order; obedience to them is an act of conscience, not merely to evade punishment. Citizens shall also pay their taxes and pay respect and honor to their rulers. Civil disobedience provokes God's wrath. The primary obedience, however, is due to Christ, who is "the ruler of the kings of the earth" (Rev. 1:5). It is only when civil authorities order something that contradicts the will of Christ that they shall be denied obedience, even at the risk of punishment and death. John is not attacking the state as such but only that part of the system, based on negative values, that hinders full observance of gospel values.

Christians are therefore uncomfortable witnesses to Christ towards a world whose set of values often belongs to the anti-kingdom. This is evident in Revelation 11:1-13, where two olive trees and two lampstands represent the prophetic witness of believers (cf. Zech. 4:2-3, 11-14). They are endowed with the same power Moses and Aaron had, and protected by God, but demonic forces will have them killed and the world will rejoice and feast over their disappearance, for their constant denouncing witness had exasperated all those who followed the ways of the anti-kingdom. Their bodies will even be denied burial, but, to everyone's astonishment and terror, they will be raised again after three days and a half, like their Lord, and taken up to heaven, and the world's apparent victory will turn into mourning.

Chapter 12 introduces the figure of "a woman clothed with the sun, with the moon under her feet, and on her head a crown of twelve stars. She was pregnant and was crying out in birth pangs, and in the agony of giving birth. . . . She gave birth to a son, a male child, who is to rule all the nations with a rod of iron. But her child was snatched away and taken to God and to his throne" (12:1-2, 5). This is usually interpreted as the ideal Israel, represented by the mother of Jesus and later transformed into the church. Her opponent is the great red dragon with his angels who battle with and are defeated by Michael and his angels; but the victory is due to "the blood of the Lamb and by the word of their [Christians'] testimony, for they did not cling to life even in the face of death" (12:11). This is both the beginning of the end and the end of the beginning, for the conflict will continue throughout history.

Revelation 17 presents Rome and the empire as the great whore with whom all the kings of the earth committed fornication by accepting the terms of her services. She is also Babylon, Israel's traditional enemy, doomed to be destroyed by the Lamb, "Lord of lords and King of kings" (17:14), and his elect. The fall of Babylon the whore and the lamentations of her lovers are described in beautiful poetic verse in Revelation 18.

The seer now passes on to raise the hope of Christians who are suffering the tribulations of their adverse historical predicament. After the destruction of Babylon, Christ, the Word of God, takes the situation in hand; he defeats the beast and the antichrist (19:17-21) and casts them into the lake of fire. The resurrection takes place and everyone is called to judgment according to his works, faith, and perseverance. "The last enemy to be destroyed is death," Paul had said (1 Cor. 15:26), and John repeats this by his assurance that the dragon,

Satan, and death itself will also be thrown down into the lake of fire. The sovereign of the anti-kingdom, his minions, and death, his accomplice, are now no more. The Word of God restores everything to life, which was in him from the very beginning (John 1:2-4).

The subject of judgment and resurrection belongs to what is usually called consequent eschatology, that is, what is to take place at the end of the ages. Yet the book of Revelation is mostly realized eschatology, the saving and judging power of the risen Christ within history. This follows the Johannine tradition of an "eternal life" which the believer possesses in the present and which will reach its perfection in the hereafter.

In Revelation 21 enters Jerusalem, Babylon's counterpart, bride and spouse of the Lamb. Jerusalem is at the same time a city, the church, God's holy temple, and paradise, images that merge into one another from Revelation 20 onwards. It is the final act in the great drama of the Apocalypse.

> Then I saw a new heaven and a new earth; for the first heaven and the first earth had passed away, and the sea [= chaos] was no more. And I saw the holy city, the new Jerusalem, coming down out of heaven from God, prepared as a bride adorned for her husband. And I heard a loud voice from the throne saying, "See, the home of God is among mortals. He will dwell with them as their God; they will be his peoples, and God himself will be with them; he will wipe every tear from their eyes. Death will be no more; mourning and crying and pain will be no more, for the first things have passed away." (21:1-4)

The repetition of the covenant formula in this passages means that the new covenant predicted by Jeremiah (31:31-34) has now come to pass. The new Jerusalem come down from heaven, from God, the complete fulfillment of the new covenant, is the Father's nuptial gift to his Son. History has been wrapped up and forgotten; only life eternal reigns.

The image of a city-bride is indeed strange. It makes sense if we conceive it as the empire the Lord God bequeaths to the Lamb, the King of kings and the Lord of lords. She is at the same time his domain and the object of his loving care.

The Lamb-Bride motif had its foundation in the depiction of Israel as Yahweh's bride in Hosea and Ezekiel 16. Ephesians takes up the church-Christ relationship as the model of Christian marriage: "Husbands, love your wives, just as Christ loved the church and gave himself up for her, in order to make her holy by cleansing her by the washing of water by the word, so as to present the church to himself in splendor, without a spot or wrinkle or anything of the kind — yes, so that she may be holy and without blemish. . . . This is a great mystery, and I am applying it to Christ and the church" (Eph. 5:25-27, 32).

The radiant city-church is composed of the twelve tribes of Israel founded on the twelve apostles (21:11-14); she is the perfect fulfillment of the first covenant inaugurated on Sinai. The author can only describe her radiance by making use of all the precious stones in his knowledge. We shall let the text speak for itself:

> And the street of the city is pure gold, transparent as glass. I saw no temple in the city, for its temple is the Lord God the Almighty and the Lamb. And the city has no need of sun or moon to shine on it, for the glory of God is its light, and its lamp is the Lamb. The nations will walk by its light, and the kings of the earth will bring their glory into it. Its gates will never be shut by day — and there will be no night there. People will bring into it the glory and the honor of the nations. But nothing unclean will enter it, nor anyone who practices abomination or falsehood, but only those who are written in the Lamb's book of life. Then the angel showed me the river of the water of life, bright as crystal, flowing from the throne of God and of the Lamb through the middle of the street of the city. On either side of the river, is the tree of life with its twelve

kinds of fruit, producing its fruit each month; and the leaves of the tree are for the healing of the nations. Nothing accursed will be found there any more. But the throne of God and of the Lamb will be in it, and his servants will worship him; they will see his face, and his name will be on their foreheads. And there will be no more night; they need no light of lamp or sun, for the Lord God will be their light, and they will reign for ever and ever. (21:21b–22:5)

The Apocalypse, with all its plagues, earthquakes, and monsters, is not meant to scare the believer. The communities to which it was addressed had enough to scare them in their daily lives, being persecuted by both Jews and Gentiles. The seer's message is one of assurance and hope, not only in spite of present suffering, but through this suffering, which mingles their blood with the redeeming blood of the Lamb. It is the word that sustained martyrs and confessors throughout the ages, and speaks to each one of us today in whatever historical circumstance we find ourselves in. There have been, still are, and always will be many Babylons in the course of history whose fall is followed by songs of lament or joy. Jerusalem, the church, survives, continually being purified from her human imperfections, until she reaches the ideal splendor of a bride worthy to be presented to the risen Christ, King of kings and Lord of lords. To understand the moment of history in which we live, it is necessary to pray with the Scriptures in one hand and the newspaper in the other. It is what John the seer did to produce his book.

Conclusion

This overview of the various strands of spirituality in the New Testament should clarify the problem we posed in the introduction about what we exactly mean by "spirituality." If we consider it as the believer's full response to God's offer of salvation in Christ, then much depends on the model of salvation elaborated by each author in the New Testament. These models constitute a "theology"; hence we can speak of Pauline or Johannine theologies. They are partial because they are only a fraction of the complete concept of God and Christ either Paul or John preached to their communities. What they wrote was only what was required by the circumstance and purpose of their message. In the New Testament canon these theological strands intertwine like the various melodic strands in a polyphonic motet to produce a symphony of voices, and so do the moral responses they propose. This means that we cannot relegate spirituality to a mere moral response. *Metanoia* means a complete change of mentality, a new outlook on life based on the Christ-event, and that changed outlook will reflect the degree to which our faith has transformed our *Weltanschauung*. Apart from the observance of God's commandments, dynamic and yet contemplative spirituality also involves prayer, good works, an ecclesial and apostolic conscience, and social action, all prompted and animated by the love the Holy Spirit gives us. In short, it means making the first three requests of the Our Father — Hallowed be thy name, thy kingdom come, and thy will be done — the principal purpose of our existence. Spirituality requires that prayerful meditation which will personalize our faith and make it part of our personality. We may be more attracted by Paul's or Matthew's presentation of the Christian message, and lay the accent on specific spiritual attitudes, but each of the authors we examined is a facet of the jewel of God's saving love; and love is only requited by love. Hence the depth of the spiritual stance of each individual will depend on his or her appreciation of the gift of faith he or she is endowed with, and on the degree of gratitude God's gift in Christ arouses in each one of us.